Microsoft® Internet Explorer 4.0

Timothy J. O'Leary
Arizona State University

Linda I. O'Leary

Irwin
McGraw-Hill

Boston   Burr Ridge, IL   Dubuque, IA   Madison, WI   New York   San Francisco   St. Louis
Bangkok   Bogotá   Caracas   Lisbon   London   Madrid
Mexico City   Milan   New Delhi   Seoul   Singapore   Sydney   Taipei   Toronto

Irwin/McGraw-Hill

*A Division of The **McGraw·Hill** Companies*

Microsoft ® Internet Explorer 4.0

Copyright © 1999 by The McGraw-Hill Companies, Inc. All rights reserved. Printed in the United States of America. Except as permitted under the United States Copyright Act of 1976, no part of this publication may be reproduced or distributed in any form or by any means, or stored in a data base or retrieval system, without the prior written permission of the publisher.

This book is printed on acid-free paper.

2 3 4 5 6 7 8 9 0 BAN BAN 9 0 0 9

ISBN 0-07-228534-6

Vice President and Editorial Director: Michael W. Junior
Sponsoring Editor: Rhonda Sands
Developmental Editor: Kyle Thomes
Marketing Manager: Jodi McPherson
Senior Project Manager: Beth Cigler
Manager, New Book Production: Melonie Salvati
Art Director: Francis Owens
Senior Designer: Lorna Lo
Supplement Coordinator: Jennifer L. Frazier
Project Manager: Beth Cigler
Compositor: GTS Graphics, Inc.
Typeface: 10/13 ITC Clearface Regular
Printer: The Banta Book Group

Library of Congress Cataloging-in-Publication Data

O'Leary, Timothy J., 1947–
   Microsoft Internet Explorer 4.0 / Timothy J. O'Leary, Linda
     I. O'Leary.
       p.   cm.
   Includes index.
   ISBN 0-07-228534-6
     1. Microsoft Internet Explorer.   2. Internet (Computer network)
  3. World Wide Web (information retrieval system)   I. O'Leary, Linda
I. II. Title.
TK5105.883.M53045   1999
005.7'13769—dc21   98-27515

http://www.mhhe.com

Contents

Overview IE1
The Internet and the World Wide Web   IE1
Definition of Internet   IE1
Things You Can Do on the Internet   IE1
About the World Wide Web   IE2
How Does Information Travel on the Internet?   IE2
How Do You Connect?   IE3
Microsoft Internet Explorer 4   IE4
Internet Terminology   IE5
Case Study for Labs 1–5   IE6
Before You Begin   IE6
Instructional Conventions   IE8

Lab 1   Navigating the Web   IE8
Exploring the Browser Window   IE9
Entering a URL   IE15
Selecting Links   IE18
Using the History List   IE23
Creating and Organizing Favorites   IE26
Viewing the HTML Source Code   IE30
Saving Web Pages and Images   IE31
Using Forms   IE33
Printing Web Pages   IE35
Lab Review   IE36
   Key Terms   IE36
   Command Summary   IE36
   Matching   IE37
   Fill-In Questions   IE37
   Discussion Questions   IE39
Hands-On Practice Exercises   IE39
Concept Summary   IE44

Lab 2   Finding Information on the Web   IE46
Finding Search Services   IE47
Searching by Topic   IE51
Searching by Keyword   IE55
Advanced Searches   IE58
Using a Metasearch Engine   IE63
Finding People and Businesses   IE66
Lab Review   IE69
   Key Terms   IE69
   Command Summary   IE69
   Matching   IE69
   Fill-In Questions   IE70
   Discussion Questions   IE70
Hands-On Practice Exercises   IE71
Concept Summary   IE74

Lab 3   Corresponding Using E-Mail   IE76
What Is E-Mail?   IE77
Setting Up Outlook Express   IE78
Composing an E-Mail Message   IE83
Checking Spelling   IE89
Editing a Message   IE91
Formatting a Message   IE92
Attaching Files   IE93
Sending a Message   IE94
Opening an Attachment   IE94
Checking Incoming Mail   IE96
Creating an Address Book   IE100
Replying to E-Mail   IE103
Forwarding a Message   IE104

Saving a Message   IE107
Deleting a Message   IE107
Printing a Message   IE108
Lab Review   IE108
   Key Terms   IE108
   Command Summary   IE109
   Matching   IE110
   Fill-In Questions   IE111
   Discussion Questions   IE111
Hands-On Practice Exercises   IE112
Concept Summary   IE114

Lab 4   Communicating with Newsgroups, Mailing Lists, and Chat Groups   IE116

Finding and Subscribing to Newsgroups   IE117
Reading Newsgroup Messages   IE123
Posting a Message to a Newsgroup   IE125
Replying to a Newsgroup Message   IE130
Unsubscribing to Newsgroups   IE131
Searching for Newsgroup Topics   IE131
Finding Mailing Lists   IE132
Subscribing to Mailing Lists   IE135
Joining a Chat Discussion   IE140
Lab Review   IE143
   Key Terms   IE143
   Command Summary   IE143
   Matching   IE144
   Fill-In Questions   IE144
   Discussion Questions   IE145
Hands-On Practice Exercises   IE146
Concept Summary   IE150

Lab 5   Creating Web Pages   IE152

Designing a Web Page   IE153
Entering the Page Content   IE156
Formatting Text   IE158
Aligning Paragraphs   IE159
Applying Character Effects   IE161
Adding a Background   IE163
Inserting Images   IE166
Previewing the Page   IE169
Adding Lines   IE171
Creating a Bulleted List   IE173
Creating Links   IE174
Publishing a Web Page   IE179
Lab Review   IE180
   Key Terms   IE180
   Command Summary   IE180
   Matching   IE181
   Fill-In Questions   IE182
   Discussion Questions   IE182
Hands-On Practice Exercises   IE182
Concept Summary   IE184

Appendix   Additional Internet Tools: FTP and Telnet   IE186

File Transfer Protocol   IE186
Using FTP   IE189
Telnet   IE191
Using Telnet   IE191
Lab Review   IE196
   Key Terms   IE196
   Matching   IE196
   Discussion Questions   IE196
Hands-On Practice Exercises   IE197

Glossary of Key Terms   IE199

Command Summary   IE205

Index   IE209

Overview

The Internet and the World Wide Web

Every day you see references to the Internet in the newspaper, in TV ads, in popular soaps and sitcoms, and more. You would need to be living in the backwoods not to hear or see references to such things as e-mail. What does all this mean to you? It means that in the future how you learn, do business, shop, or play will be different. Through the Internet you will find amusement, companionship, information, and tremendous opportunity. In the future, not knowing how to use the Internet will have an effect similar to not knowing how to read today.

Definition of Internet

What is the Internet? It is a network of thousands of computer networks that allows computers to communicate with each other. The popular term for the Internet is the "information highway." Like a highway, the Internet connects thousands of computers throughout the world, making available more information than you could read in a lifetime.

In 1993 the Internet connected 45,000 networks. Today's estimates are that between 2 and 4 million computers in 156 countries are connected to the Internet, and that 25 to 35 million people have access to the Internet. In the United States alone 7 to 15 million people have access. The Internet is expected to continue growing from about 3.2 million computers today to over 100 million machines on all 6 continents. By 2000 there will be an estimated 1 million networks connecting 1 billion users, with the majority of these users to be through at-home connections.

Things You Can Do on the Internet

The uses for the Internet are many and varied, and include the following:

- Send and receive electronic mail (e-mail). The largest use of the Internet is to send e-mail messages between users. E-mail is the process that allows you to send and receive messages along Internet pathways to and from users at other computer sites.

- Transfer files between computers. File Transfer Protocol or FTP allows you to send (upload) or receive (download) files between computers. The files are made available on the hard drives of computers and are similar to an electronic library of information that can be accessed through the Internet by all users.

- Interact with other computers. Telnet is software that gives a user the ability to log on to another computer and run programs. It is also a utility that lets you run other search or information services. Other "client software" is available if you have Windows or a Mac that connects you to a search service but does not use Telnet.

- Participate in discussion groups. Newsgroups are databases of messages on a huge number of topics. Users participate in public discussions about the topic by sending e-mail messages to the newsgroup. Mailing lists are another type of discussion group, consisting of a database of people interested in a particular topic. Your e-mail messages are mailed to the address of every participant in the mailing list. Chat groups, another type of discussion group, allow people to converse in real time.

- Search the World Wide Web. The World Wide Web, also called the WWW or Web, allows users to quickly jump from one information source to another related source. These sources of information may be on the same computer or different computers around the world.

About the World Wide Web

The World Wide Web consists of information organized into pages that contain text and graphic images. But most importantly, a page contains hypertext links, or highlighted keywords and images, that lead to related information. Clicking on the links quickly transports you to the location where that information is stored. The links may take you to other pages, text files, graphic images, movies, or audio clips. The Web allows users to view millions of pages of information by jumping from one related source to another by clicking on links.

To access the WWW, you must have a browser software program. Browsers display text and images, access FTP sites, and provide in one tool an uncomplicated interface to the Internet and WWW documents. Browsers allow you to surf the net unencumbered by the complexity of how to access information on the Internet. Two popular browser programs are Microsoft's Internet Explorer and Netscape's Communicator.

How Does Information Travel on the Internet?

The Internet uses a standard set of protocols, or rules for communication between computers. Protocols are a set of rules that establish guidelines for methods of communication to ensure uniformity among users. This allows various computer systems to connect and communicate.

Transmission Control Protocol/Internet Protocol (TCP/IP) is the core protocol used on the Internet. It breaks the information that is being transmitted into small packets of several hundred bytes each, including the addresses of sending and receiving computers. Each packet travels independently to its destination. The packets are sent along the network until they reach a router. Routers are the switchers of the system and are located at network intersections. Routers determine the best (fastest, most direct, least crowded) path for the packet to travel to reach its destination. There are many different paths to the same destination. As packets arrive at the destination, they are reassembled (they may arrive out of sequence). If a packet arrives damaged, it is requested to be sent again from the host. When reassembled, the source and destination address information are removed. The use of small packets helps the network to operate efficiently, so that load is distributed over the entire network, thereby avoiding overburdening any one part of the network.

Other protocols that are used are Point to Point Protocol (PPP) and Serial Line Internet Protocol (SLIP). PPP creates an Internet connection that checks data transfer over lines and resends the data if damaged. SLIP is similar to PPP, but does not provide damage check.

How Do You Connect?

Many schools and businesses have direct access to the Internet using special high-speed communication lines and equipment. Students and employees are typically provided access through the organization's local area network (LAN) or through personal computers acting as dumb terminals (a terminal that attaches directly to a mainframe or other large computer).

Another way to access the Internet is through an Internet Service Provider (ISP) such as America Online and Microsoft Network. To access the ISP, you use your personal computer, modem, and telecommunications software to log onto the online service. Your computer is the client that links to a larger computer called the server, which runs special software that provides access to the Internet. You pay a fee for use of their service.

You may have free access to the Internet through a nearby city, college, or corporation. The level of access through these sources varies, as explained below.

- *Local Bulletin Board Systems (BBS).* Many BBS's have limited access to the Internet, commonly e-mail, mailing lists, and newsgroups, and do not offer nearly the amount of information as is available through the Internet. Also, many offer information on specialized topics only. You can find BBS telephone numbers through computer magazines and local computer newsletters.

- *Campus Computer Systems.* If you are affiliated with a college or university with an internal computer network that is connected to the Internet, you may be able to get "free" access (no charge directly to you—however, someone is paying). Access from outside the organization is generally via modem.

- *Corporate Network.* If you are affiliated with a corporation that is connected to the Internet, you may be able to get "free" access, generally via modem, similar to campus computer systems.

INTERNET EXPLORER 4

- *Libraries.* College and university libraries and many public libraries have replaced card catalogs with computer terminals tied to a central database. When colleges and universities connected to the Internet, the libraries were easily able to make their databases available. If they have the funds, public libraries may provide access to the Internet through their computer network.

- *Freenets.* Freenets are community-based bulletin boards whose area of concern is community related. All have the same basic structure in that they are set up like an electronic town. The setup allows you to stop at different "buildings" to collect information about the community. Users must register to use the freenet. This is usually free to the community resident. Also, you can register as a guest, which allows you to look around and explore the freenet with limited access time. Freenets are directly accessible by modem (you need to locate the phone number). Some freenets also provide access to the Internet.

Microsoft Internet Explorer 4

Microsoft Internet Explorer 4 is a browser suite that comes in a Standard version and a Full version along with a browser-only version. The Standard version includes the six components described below.

Component	Use
4.01 Browser	Browse the WWW
Java Support	Enables you to create and run Java applets from a Web site
Microsoft Outlook Express	Send and receive e-mail
True Web integration	Opens other programs within Internet Explorer
Microsoft Wallet	Stores address and payment method information on a personal computer for use in online shopping transactions

The Full version includes the additional components described below.

Component	Use
Microsoft Netmeeting	Hold conferences over the Web or a local area network
Netshow	An audio and video system for the Web
FrontPage Express	Used to create and publish Web pages
Microsoft Web Publishing Wizard	Step-by-step creation of web pages
Microsoft Chat 2.0	Chat with others in a chat room, in graphical comic-strip format or standard text format

Internet Terminology

browser: A software program used to access and display WWW pages.

download: To copy or receive a file from another computer using FTP.

e-mail: The process that allows you to send and receive messages along Internet pathways to and from users at other computer sites.

FTP: File Transfer Protocol allows you to upload or download files between computers.

hypertext link: A connection to another Web page or to another location on the current page.

Internet: A network of thousands of computer networks that allows computers to communicate with each other.

ISP: An Internet Service Provider is a company that provides access to the Internet for a fee.

mailing list: A discussion group in which e-mail messages are sent directly to the e-mail address of every participant in the mailing list.

newsgroup: A discussion group in which e-mail messages are stored on centralized computer sites.

PPP: Point to Point Protocol creates an Internet connection that checks data transfer over lines and sends it again if damaged.

protocol: A set of rules that establishes guidelines for methods of communication between computers to ensure uniformity among users.

router: A switch located at a network intersection on the Internet that determines the best path for a packet to travel to reach its destination.

SLIP: Serial Line Internet Protocol is similar to PPP, but does not provide damage check.

TCP/IP: Transmission Control Protocol/Internet Protocol is the core protocol used on the Internet.

Telnet: A software program that gives users the ability to log on to another computer and run programs.

upload: To send a file to another computer using FTP.

WWW: The World Wide Web is a part of the Internet that consists of information organized into pages containing text and graphic images and hypertext links.

Case Study for Labs 1–5

As a recent college graduate, you have accepted your first job as a management trainee for The Sports Company, a chain of discount sporting goods stores located in large metropolitan areas throughout the United States. The management trainee program emphasis is on computer applications in the area of retail management and requires that you work in several areas of the company.

In this series of labs, you are working in the marketing department. You have recently helped with setting up The Sports Company Web site. As part of your continued involvement in this project, you are using Internet Explorer 4 to find information, send e-mail, and create a Web page.

Lab 1. The first lab introduces you to Microsoft Internet Explorer's browser. You will learn basic techniques for navigating the WWW and how to save and print pages.

Lab 2. This lab continues with the browser component and demonstrates how to use the search features to make finding information on the WWW much easier and more efficient.

Lab 3. In this lab you use Microsoft Outlook Express to compose, send, reply to, forward, and delete e-mail messages. In addition, you learn how to create a personal address book.

Lab 4. This lab continues with Microsoft Outlook Express, through which you learn how to find, read, and communicate with newsgroups. You will also learn how to subscribe and unsubscribe to a mailing list. In addition, you will learn how to use Microsoft's Chat 2.0 to participate in an online discussion.

Lab 5. In the last lab you use FrontPage Express to create a Web page.

Appendix. Finally, the Appendix gives a short demonstration of two additional Internet tools: FTP and Telnet.

Before You Begin

To the Student

The following resources are needed to complete these labs:

- The full version of Microsoft Internet Explorer 4 must be installed on your computer system. If the version of Internet Explorer 4 you are using is different than that used in this book, the menu selections and instructions in this manual may be slightly different.

- You need to have an Internet account with your school and an e-mail address.

- The data files required to complete this series of labs are provided by your instructor and should be copied to a new floppy disk.

- It is helpful if you are already familiar with how to use Windows applications.

In addition, you will learn while using the WWW that it is in a state of constant change. One day you can connect to a site and the next day you cannot. The information on a site may change from week to week. New sites are added and others are removed. There is no guarantee that the information you found one day will be there the next, but you may just as easily find something new. Because things constantly change on the Internet, you need to be open to trying and searching. You may get lost, but you can always get home.

To the Instructor

The following assumptions have been made:

- The figures in this lab were created using a Standard VGA setting (640 x 480). If the screen display settings at your school are 800 x 600 or higher, more information will be displayed in a maximized window than shown in the figures in the text.

- The Full version of Internet Explorer 4 is installed on your computer system.

- The Outlook Express preferences are cleared when Outlook Express is exited. This allows the Internet Connection Wizard to appear when Outlook Express is first accessed. If your setup is different and the wizard does not appear, students will need to set their preferences using Tools/Accounts. Students will need e-mail addresses prior to setting Outlook Express preferences. Some systems allow the preferences to be saved for each student. If this is the case at your school, students will not need to re-enter their preferences each time they use Outlook Express.

- The default preferences are in effect each time Internet Explorer, Outlook Express, and FrontPage Express are loaded. It is particularly important that the following settings be in effect:

Internet Explorer:

- The Text Labels for the Standard Buttons toolbar are on.
- The Address Bar and Links Bar share the same row.
- The option "Internet Explorer should check to see whether it is the default browser" is cleared (View/Internet Options/Programs).

Outlook Express:

- Send Messages Immediately is on.
- Include Message in Reply is on.
- AutoComplete E-mail Addresses is on.

- Accessing Telnet through Internet Explorer requires that Internet Explorer be appropriately configured.

Instructional Conventions

This text uses the following instructional conventions:

- Steps that you are to perform are preceded with a bullet (■) and are in blue type.

- Command sequences you are to issue appear following the word "Choose." Each menu command selection is separated by a /. If the menu command can be selected by typing a letter of the command, the letter will appear bold and underlined.

- Commands that can be initiated using a button and the mouse appear following the word "Click." The menu equivalent and keyboard shortcut appear in a margin note when the action is first introduced.

- Anything you are to type appears in bold text.

INTERNET EXPLORER 4

Navigating the Web

COMPETENCIES

After completing this lab, you will know how to:

1. Enter a URL.
2. Select links.
3. Use the History list.
4. Create and organize Favorites.
5. View the HTML source code.
6. Save Web pages and images.
7. Use a form.
8. Print Web pages.

CASE STUDY

The Sports Company has recently decided to take advantage of the Internet by creating a site on the World Wide Web (WWW) to market their products and advertise the company. In addition to the traditional commercial aspects of the site, such as a catalog of products, online order forms, and location information, they have included the first issue of *The Sports Company Update,* the monthly newsletter, to provide customers with health- and fitness-related information.

Your supervisor has asked you to look at the online newsletter and to make suggestions for improvements that would take better advantage of the Web.

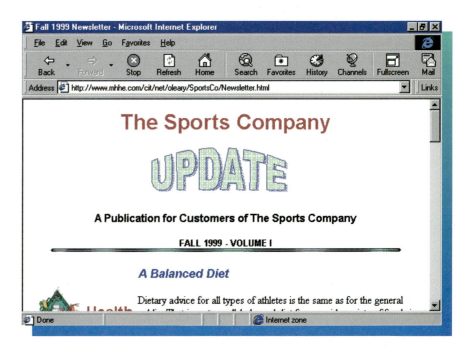

Concept Overview

The following concepts will be introduced in this lab:

1. **Web Page** — A Web page is a text file that has been created using a special programming language, called HyperText Markup Language, and that contains links to other Web pages and graphics. *HTML*

2. **Uniform Resource Locator** — A Uniform Resource Locator (URL) provides location information that is used to navigate through the Internet to access a page.

3. **Hypertext Link** — A hypertext link, also called a hyperlink or simply a link, is a connection to another Web page or to another location on the current page.

4. **Frame** — Frames divide the Web browser's display into windows. Each window is a frame that can contain a separate, scrollable page.

5. **Cache** — A cache is a location in your computer system that stores the page information when it is downloaded from the network. *memory downloaded*

6. **Favorite** — A favorite permanently stores the URL of a page so that you can easily access the page again by selecting the favorite from the Favorites list.

7. **HyperText Markup Language** — All Web pages are written using a programming language called HyperText Markup Language (HTML).

8. **Security** — Security is low on transmissions of information over the Internet. To make transmissions secure, certificates, encryption, decryption, and digital signatures are used.

Exploring the Browser Window

To view the newsletter on the WWW, you will use the Microsoft Internet Explorer 4 (IE4) browser program. A **browser** program is used to move to and display information located on the WWW.

- If necessary, turn on your computer.
- Double-click [Internet Explorer icon] Internet Explorer.

If a Dial-up Connection dialog box appears, you will need to provide the required information to establish your Internet connection. This may require that you enter a user name and password.

- If necessary, enter the information needed by your school to establish your Internet connection.
- Click [Connect].

If the Internet Explorer 4 shortcut is not on your desktop, choose [Start] / Programs/Internet Explorer/Internet Explorer to load the program, or follow the directions provided by your school.

If you are using Windows 98 in Web style view, single click [Internet Explorer icon].

INTERNET EXPLORER 4

IE10 Navigating the Web

Your screen should be similar to Figure 1-1.

FIGURE 1-1

> If necessary, click 🗖 to maximize the window.

The Internet Explorer 4 browser window is displayed on your screen. The information displayed in the window will most likely be different than that shown in Figure 1-1. Your screen will probably display information about your school. This is because Internet Explorer can be customized to display on startup different information than is specified in the program's setup procedure. In a few moments you will learn how to change the information displayed in Internet Explorer so that it is the same as the figures in the text. Even though at present your screen displays different information, the components of the browser window are the same.

As in other Windows 98 applications, the window has a title bar, Minimize ▬ and Maximize/Restore buttons 🗗, Close button ✕, menu bar, toolbars, status bar, and scroll bars. The large center area of the window is the **main window** where the contents of a Web page are displayed.

Concept 1: Web Page

A **Web page** is a text file that has been created using a special programming language called HyperText Markup Language, and that contains links to other Web pages and graphics. The Web page is stored on a computer called a **server**, where it can be accessed and displayed using a browser program. A server may contain several Web sites. A **Web site** consists of interconnected pages that have a common theme and design. Each Web page is designed by the people at the Web site and will contain information unique to that site.

Web pages are different from other types of text documents in two ways. First, they are interactive. This means the user can send information or commands to the Web site, which control a program running on the Web server, and receive a response from the site. Second, Web pages can use multimedia. This includes the ability to add animation to a page, display video, and run audio files.

When Internet Explorer first loads, it displays the **startup home page.** This is a page that the Internet Explorer program has been set to load by default. As mentioned earlier, most likely this is your school's home page. A **home page** is the first page of information for a Web site. Generally home pages include a brief welcome with information about the site and a table of contents that will take you to other pages of information within the Web site.

The title bar displays the name of the page you are currently viewing. The six pull-down menus below the title bar when selected display Internet Explorer (IE) commands that allow you to control the screen appearance and how IE performs, as well as provide Help information and general file utilities such as saving and printing. The general features in each menu are described below.

Menu	Use
File	Used to open, save, print, and perform other tasks related to files as well as provide a list of the last visited sites.
Edit	Used to cut, copy, paste, and search within the displayed window.
View	Controls the display of onscreen features such as toolbars, fonts, page content, and page information.
Go	Used to navigate among pages and to open supplementary applications.
Favorites	Lists of user-defined favorite sites.
Help	Provides documentation and support services for using Internet Explorer.

IE 12 Navigating the Web

On the right edge of the menu bar is the Internet Explorer company logo . Clicking will display Internet Explorer's home page. It also animates whenever a page transfer is in progress. The toolbar buttons activate the most commonly used IE features. By default the three toolbars, Standard Buttons toolbar, the Links Bar, and Address Bar, are displayed when IE is first opened. Notice the move handle to the left of each toolbar. Dragging the move handle up or down allows you to change the order of the toolbars. If multiple toolbars share the same row, dragging the move handle left or right adjusts the size of the toolbar. If you right-click on a toolbar, the toolbar shortcut menu is displayed. Using this menu you can specify which toolbars are displayed and turn on or off the display of the button labels to allow more space to display page content. You will try out several of these features.

> The logo may be another company's logo (such as an Internet service provider), and clicking on it will take you to that organization's home page.

- Right-click on the menu bar or any toolbar to display the shortcut menu.

All four options should be preceded with a ✔, indicating they are enabled.

- If necessary, choose any options that are not preceded with a ✔ to turn them on.
- Choose **T**ext Labels from the toolbar shortcut menu.

> The menu equivalent is **V**iew/**T**oolbars/**T**ext Labels.

Now the buttons on the Standard Buttons toolbar are smaller in size and do not display the button name. You can display the button name by pointing to the button.

- Point to any button on the Standard Buttons toolbar to see the ToolTip displaying the button name.

- Choose Text Labels from the toolbar shortcut menu to redisplay the button names.

> The menu equivalent is **V**iew/**T**oolbars/**S**tandard Buttons.

- Display the toolbar shortcut menu again and choose Standard Buttons to hide the toolbar.
- Redisplay the toolbar.

- Point to the of any toolbar and drag it up or down to move it to a new position.
- Rearrange the toolbars until each occupies a separate row.

> The mouse pointer appears as ↔ when you point to the of any toolbar, and as ✥ when you click on it to drag the toolbar to move and size it.

- Move the Links Bar into the Standard Buttons row.
- Drag the of the Links Bar to the right or left until it occupies approximately half the row space.
- Double-click the of the Links Bar to size it.

> When a toolbar is not fully displayed, you can use ◄ or ► to scroll additional buttons into view.

- Move the toolbars into the position and size as shown in Figure 1-1.

As you can see, by hiding and moving toolbars and changing the text label display, you can customize the appearance of the toolbars and minimize the space they use.

The Standard Buttons toolbar buttons, described below, are shortcuts for the most widely used commands, including those used to navigate among pages.

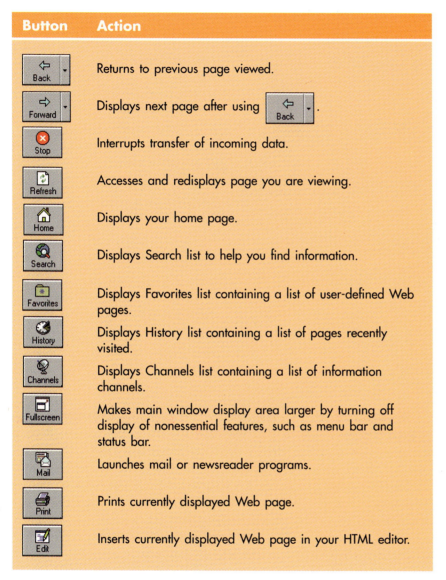

Button	Action
Back	Returns to previous page viewed.
Forward	Displays next page after using Back.
Stop	Interrupts transfer of incoming data.
Refresh	Accesses and redisplays page you are viewing.
Home	Displays your home page.
Search	Displays Search list to help you find information.
Favorites	Displays Favorites list containing a list of user-defined Web pages.
History	Displays History list containing a list of pages recently visited.
Channels	Displays Channels list containing a list of information channels.
Fullscreen	Makes main window display area larger by turning off display of nonessential features, such as menu bar and status bar.
Mail	Launches mail or newsreader programs.
Print	Prints currently displayed Web page.
Edit	Inserts currently displayed Web page in your HTML editor.

The Print and Edit buttons are displayed only when Text Labels are off if your screen resolution is 640 x 480.

The Address Bar contains the Address text box where you enter the WWW address location of a page you want to display in the main window. Currently the address for your home page is displayed. You will learn more about Web addresses shortly.

The Links Bar initially contains buttons that access various Microsoft pages designed to help you locate information. This toolbar can be customized to display buttons to your favorite locations on the Web. The default buttons are described in the table below.

■ Expand the Links Bar to see the buttons, then return it to its original size.

> Your Links Bar may display a different combination of the links described here.

Button	Action
Best of the Web	Accesses Site of the Day, Find It Fast, and Best of the Web, which provide good starting points to locating information on the Internet.
Internet Start or Today's Link	Accesses Microsoft's start page containing news, stock quotes, and other current topics.
Internet Explorer News or Product News	Accesses Explorer product news and new software applications to enhance Explorer.
Channel Guide	Accesses frequently updated page of links to selected sites.
Customize Links	Accesses page containing links to multimedia elements used when creating a Web page.
Web Gallery	Accesses features for authoring and Web site administration.
Microsoft	Accesses Microsoft's home page.

The status bar below the main window area contains a status message area, progress bar, and a security level indicator. The status message area displays various messages, such as advising you of the progress of a page as it is downloaded to your computer. The progress bar illustrates the transfer's progress. The bar fills as the page is loaded. The security level indicator currently displays the default security level setting, Internet zone. Internet Explorer includes four categories into which you can assign Web sites. Each category can have different security settings associated with it that control how information from that site is handled by your system. The Internet zone setting controls the level of security for all Web sites that are not assigned another setting.

> Double-clicking the security level indicator displays a window containing information about the IE security features.

> You will learn more about Internet security later in this lab.

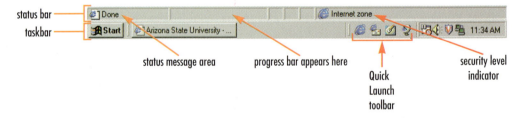

status bar — Done
taskbar — Start   Arizona State University - ...
status message area
progress bar appears here
Quick Launch toolbar
security level indicator
Internet zone   11:34 AM

Finally, below the status bar is the taskbar, which may display the Quick Launch toolbar. This toolbar consists of four buttons that are used to start Internet Explorer or Outlook Express, display the desktop, and view channels.

Entering a URL

There are several methods for browsing the WWW to view pages of information. One is to enter the URL of the page you want to view in the Address box.

> **Concept 2: Uniform Resource Locator**
>
> Each Web page has its own address, called the **Uniform Resource Locator (URL),** which provides location information used to navigate through the Internet to access a page. Although URLs appear complicated, they are actually quite easy to decipher. The URL consists of several parts specifying the protocol, server, and path name of the item. Most begin with http://www or some variation. The URL for the Arizona State University home page is:
>
>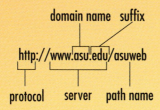
>
> The protocol identifies the type of server where the information is stored. For WWW pages, the protocol is HTTP, for HyperText Transfer Protocol. Other protocols you will see are FTP (File Transfer Protocol), NEWS (Usenet), and Gopher. A colon and two forward slashes (//) always follow the protocol. The server identifies the name of the computer system that stores the information. It typically begins with "www," indicating the site is part of the World Wide Web. The second part is the domain name, which identifies the name of the institution that owns the site. The server name also includes a suffix, which identifies the type of server. For example, the suffix .com indicates the server is a commercial server, and .edu indicates it is an educational server. The last part is the path name, which indicates where the information is located on the server. Each part of the path is preceded with a single forward slash (/).

 Refer to the Overview for a discussion of protocols.

A ~ (tilde) in a path name indicates a particular directory on the server.

Typing the URL in the Address box will take you instantly to that location. You can find URLs for many WWW sites in books, news articles, on TV, and through discussion groups. When typing a URL, you must enter it exactly, including uppercase or lowercase. However, like most browsers, Internet Explorer allows you to omit the http:// part of the URL. If the URL begins with a protocol different than http://, you must type it. You can also omit the www if the suffix is .com and the URL does not include a path name. If the URL includes a path name, you can still omit the www, but you would need to type in the suffix.

Navigating the Web

> The Address box stores the last 12 URLs that were entered.

Additionally, Internet Explorer includes an AutoComplete feature that will attempt to complete the URL for you if there is a URL that was previously entered in the Address box that matches the letters you type. If you enter an incorrect URL, an error message will appear. The following table lists some common error messages and their meanings.

Message	Meaning
DNS Lookup Failed	DNS (domain name server) is a program that exists wherever you get your Internet access. It turns the Web site address that most users see (for example, www.aol.com) into a corresponding numerical address that can be read by a computer. A DNS Lookup Failed message indicates that the browser could not contact your domain name server, or that the domain name server was not aware of the site. Make sure the domain name is not misspelled.
File Not Found	The page may no longer exist, or it may have moved to another address.
Server Error *or* Server Busy Error	The computer you are trying to contact may be offline, may have crashed, or may be busy. You might want to try again later.

The first Web site you want to see is The Sports Company's home page. The URL for this page is http://www.mhhe.com/sportsco.

> You can also use **F**ile/**O**pen or Ctrl + O to display the Open dialog box in which you enter the URL.

- Click in the Address box.
- Type **mhhe.com/sportsco**
- Press Enter.

> The current URL is highlighted and will be replaced by the new text as you type.

> You can also click ▼ in the Address box to display a menu of up to the last 12 URLs that have been entered in the Address box. Choosing a URL from the menu displays the page again.

As the content of the page that the URL refers to is transferred or downloaded from the server location to your location, the Internet Explorer company logo animates. The status message area shows information such as the total and remaining number of items being loaded and the URL. The progress bar appears and visually shows the download percentage completed. This information is important because many documents are very large and take a long time to load. When the page is fully downloaded, the status message area indicates the document transfer is complete by displaying "Done," and the Internet Explorer company logo is no longer active.

> Clicking [Stop], pressing Esc, or choosing **V**iew/**S**top will cancel a transfer immediately.

Your screen should be similar to Figure 1-2.

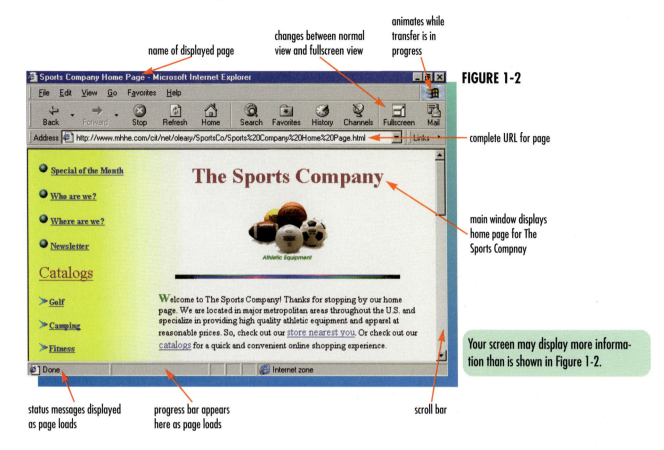

FIGURE 1-2

Your screen may display more information than is shown in Figure 1-2.

The main window displays the home page for The Sports Company, and the title bar displays the name of the current page. Notice that the Address box displays a different URL than the one you originally entered. This is because the URL you entered is a shortcut, called an **alias**, to the actual page address. The URL that is displayed is the complete URL for the page.

A scroll bar appears whenever the main window is not large enough to fully display the entire page contents. To see the rest of the page,

■ Scroll the window to the bottom of the page.

A quick way to see more of a page on the screen is to change the view to Fullscreen view.

■ Click [Fullscreen].

The menu equivalent is **V**iew/**F**ull Screen.

Your screen should be similar to Figure 1-3.

FIGURE 1-3

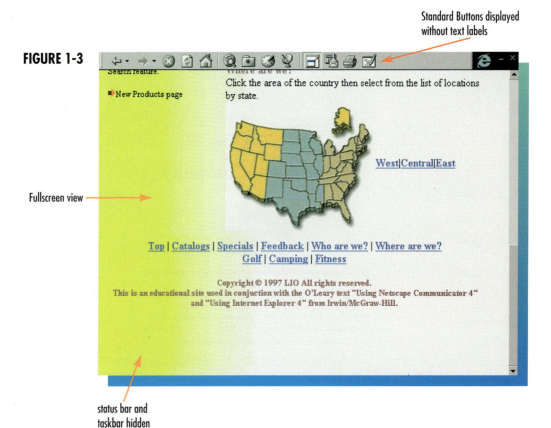

Standard Buttons displayed without text labels

Fullscreen view

status bar and taskbar hidden

This view enlarges the main window space by removing the title bar, menu bar, and all toolbars except the Standard Buttons toolbar. The Standard buttons appear without text labels to save space. In addition, the status bar and taskbars are not displayed. To return to normal view,

- Click .

Selecting Links

Probably the first thing you will notice about a page is the highlighted (underlined or colored) text. This indicates a hypertext link.

> **Concept 3: Hypertext Link**
>
> A **hypertext link,** also called a **hyperlink** or simply a **link,** is a connection to another Web page or to another location on the current page. A link most commonly appears as colored and/or underlined text. Images or icons with colored borders may also be links. Clicking on a link displays the location or page associated with the requested link.

■ Point to the Top link.

Your screen should be similar to Figure 1-4.

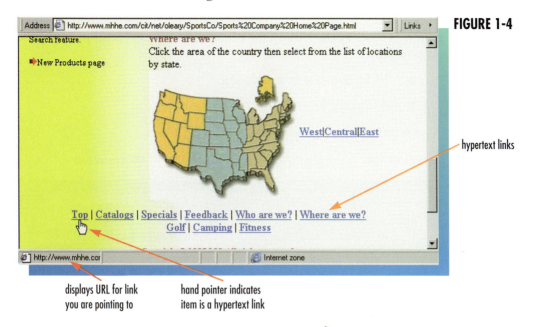

FIGURE 1-4

hypertext links

displays URL for link you are pointing to

hand pointer indicates item is a hypertext link

Notice that the mouse pointer shape changed to a hand, indicating you are pointing to a hypertext link. In addition, the URL for this link appears in the status message area.

■ Click Top.

When you click this link, the top of the home page is displayed, saving you the trouble of scrolling back to the top of the page. This type of link is most often used when a Web page is a long document.

■ Click Where are we?

Your screen should be similar to Figure 1-5.

> Click a link only once and then watch the progress bar. Clicking again cancels the first operation and starts loading the page again. Be patient.

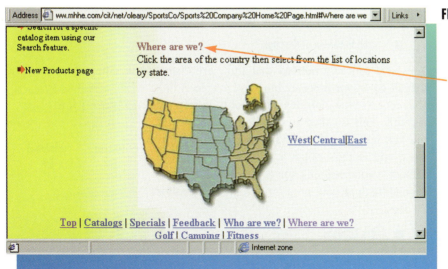

FIGURE 1-5

Clicking "Where are we?" link displays that section of the page

The section of the page appears that tells you how to find store locations. As you can see, this is much faster than scrolling.

Other links display a new page of information in the browser. When you click on a link, the location that the link refers to its transferred from the server location to your location. Watch the information in the status bar while the new page is loaded.

- Click Top to return to the top of the page.
- Click Special of the Month.

Your screen should be similar to Figure 1-6.

FIGURE 1-6

The title bar displays the name of the current page, and the Address box shows the page's URL. Next you want to see the Catalogs page.

- Scroll to bottom of the page.

You have probably noticed that links are displayed in different colors. The default colors for links are blue and purple. A link that appears blue indicates it has not been selected recently. This is called an **unfollowed link.** A purple link indicates that the link has been recently used, and is thus called a **followed link.** It will remain a followed link for a set period of time, depending upon your program setup (the default is 20 days).

- Click Catalogs.

> Many of the links on The Sports Company site may appear as followed links if a pervious user on your computer recently selected them.

Your screen should be similar to Figure 1-7.

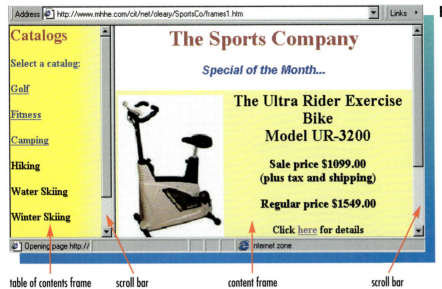

FIGURE 1-7

table of contents frame   scroll bar   content frame   scroll bar

The browser's display area is divided into two windows called frames.

> **Concept 4: Frame**
>
> **Frames** divide the Web browser's display into windows. Each window is a frame that can contain a separate, scrollable page. A group of frames is called a **frame set.** A frame set is a special Web page that defines the size and location of each window. Clicking on a frame makes it the active frame, and its URL appears in the Address box. When a frame is active, many of the toolbar and menu commands affect only the active frame. The left frame is commonly used as a table of contents to other areas in the frame set. The right frame, called the content frame, displays the contents of the selected page.
>
> Frames are used when you want the contents of one part of the Web browser's display to remain unchanged while the contents of other parts change based on hyperlinks that the user selects.

You can adjust the size of the frames by dragging the border between frames.

- Click <u>Camping</u> in the table of contents frame.
- As the page loads, scroll the content frame.

Your screen should be similar to Figure 1-8.

FIGURE 1-8

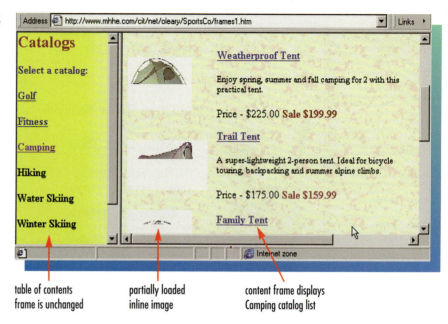

table of contents frame is unchanged
partially loaded inline image
content frame displays Camping catalog list

Information related to the topic you selected appears in the content frame. The frame on the left does not change, allowing you to quickly select a different category. Internet Explorer loads the text of a page first, followed by images. Images first appear as empty boxes containing a small image icon. As the image is loaded it replaces the box.

You probably noticed that this page took slightly longer to load. This is because it contains many pictures. Picture images are much larger in byte size than text and therefore take considerably longer to load. Usually when people design pages, they take this factor into consideration, making the images small so the page loads faster. Images that are part of a page are called **inline images,** because they load automatically as part of the page. Internet Explorer loads text first and then graphics, allowing you to read the text while the graphics continue to load.

Because the images on this page are small, this helps the page load faster, but it is difficult to see the items well. Many times an image will be a link to a page that displays the picture full size. This is called a **thumbnail** image.

- Click on the first tent thumbnail to see it full size.
- Click [Back].

> To speed up loading of pages, you can turn off loading of inline images by choosing **V**iew/Internet **O**ptions/Advanced, and then under the Multimedia section clear the Show Picture check box. Then, if you want to see the pictures on a particular page, you can right-click on the graphics and choose Show Pictures to load the graphics for that page only.

> The menu equivalent is **G**o/**B**ack, and the keyboard shortcut is [Alt] + [←].

The previously viewed page is displayed again. Likewise, clicking [Forward] will display the next page you viewed. [Forward] is only available after using [Back].

To see more information about the first-aid kit,

- Scroll the page and click First-Aid Kit.

This page provides detailed information about the item and a button to access the order page.

> The menu equivalent is **G**o/**F**orward, and the keyboard shortcut is Alt + →.

> Pointing to [Back] and [Forward] displays a ToolTip with the title of the page that will be displayed.

Using the History List

You have selected several links that have taken you to different pages of information. While you are using Internet Explorer, the program maintains a history of the places you have visited, called a **History list.** Rather than returning to a previously viewed page one at a time using the [Back] button, you can select a page you have viewed from the History list. To see the History list,

- Choose **F**ile.

The bottom section of the File menu displays a list of the page titles you have viewed since loading Internet Explorer. The most recently viewed page is at the bottom of the list. The current page is preceded with a check mark. Choosing any one of these will quickly return you to that location. As you make more selections, the older selections are removed from the History list. To return to the home page,

- Choose Sports Company Home Page.
- If necessary, move to the top of the page.

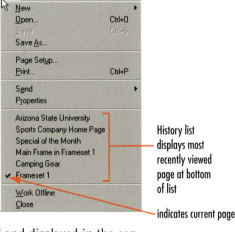

History list displays most recently viewed page at bottom of list

indicates current page

The home page for The Sports Company is reloaded and displayed in the content area. The page is not downloaded again from the server, but is reloaded from a file that was created and stored temporarily in a cache folder on your computer.

Concept 5: Cache

A **cache** is a location in your computer system that stores the page information when it is downloaded from the network. There are two types of caches, a memory cache and a disk cache. Memory cache is temporary and clears when you end your Internet Explorer session, whereas disk cache stores the page information in a folder on your hard disk that does not clear when you end your session. When the space allocated for disk cache is full, old files are cleared automatically to make space for the new information. By default Internet Explorer's disk cache location is a folder named Temporary Internet Files located in the Windows folder.

Normally, the first time you request a page, Internet Explorer retrieves the page from the network and stores the page information in both caches. If you request a page you have seen before during your current session, Internet Explorer first checks to see if the page is available in cache. If it is available, it loads the page from cache rather than the network because it is much faster and reduces network traffic.

In some cases you might not want a page to be retrieved from a cache. For example, many news service pages update the page information throughout the day, making the page you displayed initially different than the page currently offered by the network. If a modification to a particular URL has occurred, you may want the updated page rather than the old copy stored in a cache. If you click a link, choose a favorite, type a URL, or click the [Refresh] button, Internet Explorer checks with the server to see if an update has occurred before bringing a page from cache. If any change to the page has occurred, a fresh version is downloaded; otherwise a copy is quickly retrieved from cache.

If you click the [Refresh] button while holding down the [Shift] key, Internet Explorer downloads a fresh version from the network regardless of whether the page has been updated, and cache is not used. This type of reload is useful if you suspect the cached copy of a page has been corrupted or damaged during transfer.

When you click the [Back] button or choose a history item, Internet Explorer does not check the network. Since you are explicitly requesting a previously viewed page, Internet Explorer tries first to retrieve the cached copy (if still present in the cache) even if the server offers a more recent version.

You can customize cache settings using the **V**iew/Internet **O**ptions/General/Settings command. You can change the preferences to check cache every time you access the page, once per session, or never. The default setting is once per session.

> The menu equivalent is **V**iew/**R**efresh, and the keyboard shortcut is [F5].

> You will learn about favorites shortly.

Internet Explorer also maintains a more complete History list. To see this listing,

- Click [History].

> The menu equivalent is **V**iew/**E**xplorer Bar/**H**istory.

Your screen should be similar to Figure 1-9.

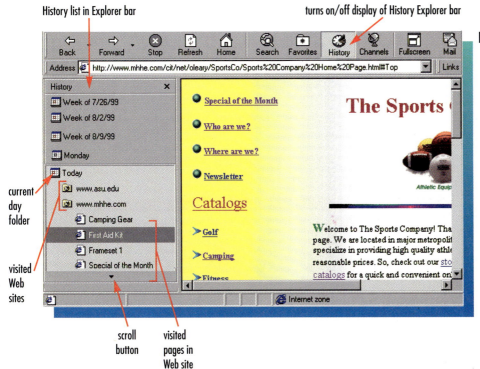

FIGURE 1-9

A frame on the left side of the screen displays the History list in the Explorer Bar. The Explorer Bar can display four different lists: Search, Favorites, History, and Channels. The History list consists of folders that categorize the history entries by week and day. The current week's entries are shown by day. To see the entries in a day or week folder, click on the folder to open it. The entries consist of Web site names. Clicking on the name opens a list of links to pages visited at that Web site. Then clicking on the link displays the page content in the frame to the right of the Explorer Bar.

As you can see, the History list includes more history links than the File menu. If the list is long, you will need to scroll the list. When you point to the bottom of the History list, a ▼ appears if the list is larger than the available space in the Explorer Bar. Clicking on this button scrolls down the list. To scroll in the opposite direction, click the ▲ at the top of the list.

- Click on the previous week's folder to display the list.
- Click on the folder again to close the list.
- Click the Today folder to display the list.
- Click the www.mhhe.com link in today's list.
- Click on the Camping Gear link and then on the Sports Company Home Page link.
- Click ☒ at the top of the Explorer Bar to close it.

> Depending on your setup, you may not have any previous day's or week's history.

> You can also click [History] again to close the Explorer Bar.

The number of days that a page is stored in the History list is determined by the length of time set in the Internet Explorer program. When the specified number of days is reached, the pages are cleared from the list.

Creating and Organizing Favorites

If you wanted to return to The Sports Company home page in a future session, you would need to retype the URL in the Address box or, if it were still available, select it from the History list. When you find a place that you would like to return to later, you can permanently store its location by making it a favorite.

> **Concept 6: Favorite**
>
> A **favorite** permanently stores the URL of a page so that you can easily access the page again by selecting the favorite from the Favorites list. The Web pages you add to the Favorites list are permanently stored on your hard disk until you delete them. Each item in the list contains the title of the page, the associated URL, and some additional date information. You can also create folders to store related favorites together. This makes the Favorites list more organized so it is easier to locate a specific Web page.

> The Favorites list is stored in c:\Windows\Favorites.

You will make The Sports Company's home page you are currently viewing a favorite.

- Choose F**a**vorites/**A**dd to Favorites.

> You can also choose Add Favorites from a page's shortcut menu to add it to the Favorites list.

The Add Favorite dialog box on your screen should be similar to Figure 1-10.

FIGURE 1-10

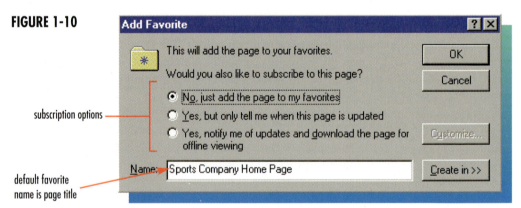

In addition to adding the page to the Favorites list, you can subscribe to the Web page. By subscribing to a page you can be notified and get updates whenever the content of the page changes. You can also give the page another name that might be more descriptive or easier to recognize than the page's real name. In this case the page's title is satisfactory. To accept the defaults and see the Web page you added to the Favorites list,

- Click OK .
- Click Favorites .

> The menu equivalent is **V**iew/**E**xplorer Bar/**F**avorites.

Your screen should be similar to Figure 1-11.

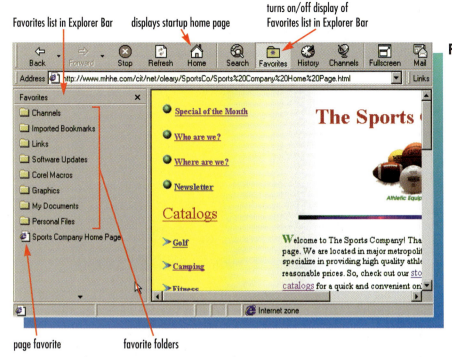

FIGURE 1-11

The Explorer Bar displays the Favorites list of all Web page favorites and folders on your computer. If this is the first time a favorite has been added to the list, there may not be any folders. Each folder is preceded with the 📁 icon. Each favorite displays the name of the page and is preceded with the 🔗 icon.

- If necessary, scroll the list to see the Sports Company Home Page favorite.

Next you will return to your startup home page and then try using the Favorites list.

- Click 🏠.
- Click the Sports Company Home Page in the Favorites list.

The page contents are reloaded. You will find creating and using favorites to be a very handy timesaver.

New favorites are added to the list in alphabetical order. As you add more favorites to your list, it is convenient to store related favorites in a folder you create or add them to an appropriate pre-existing folder. You will create a folder in which you will store the favorite you just created.

- Close the Favorites Explorer Bar.
- Choose F**a**vorites/**O**rganize Favorites.

> Pressing Ctrl + D will add the current page to the Favorites list without any further input on your part.

> Use the buttons at the top and bottom of the list to scroll.

> The menu equivalent is **G**o/**H**ome Page.

Navigating the Web

The Organize Favorites dialog box on your screen should be similar to Figure 1-12.

FIGURE 1-12

Favorite folders

page favorite

Organize button options

create new folder

This dialog box displays the contents of the Favorites folder. This is similar to how folders and files on a disk are displayed in Window's Explorer. The toolbar and Organize button options help you organize your list by allowing you to create, move, rename, and delete folders and favorites. Additionally, you can use drag and drop to rearrange your favorites. To create a new folder and move the Sports Company Home Page favorite into it,

- Click [button].
- Type your name as the folder name. [New Folder]
- Press [Enter].
- Select the Sports Company Home Page favorite and drag it to the new folder.
- Double-click the new folder to open it and see the favorite it holds.
- Click [Open].

Favorite file in folder   new folder

> As you drag, a horizontal line shows you where the favorite will be placed when you release the mouse button.

> You can also select the favorite to move, click [Move...], then select the folder name to move to.

> You could also double-click the favorite to both select it and open it in one step.

You can also create a favorite to a Web page that is not displayed. To do this,

- Right-click on the Catalogs link and choose Add to Favorites from the shortcut menu.
- Click [Create in >>].
- Select the folder with your name.

The Add Favorite dialog box should be similar to Figure 1-13.

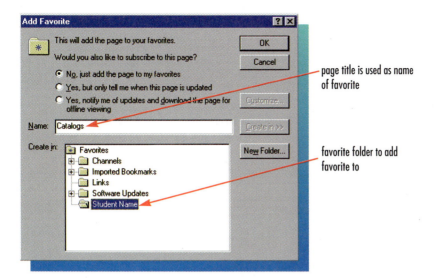

FIGURE 1-13

page title is used as name of favorite

favorite folder to add favorite to

> You can also create a new folder using this dialog box and add the favorites to it.

To add the new favorite to the list and see the two favorites in the new folder,

- Click OK .
- Click [icon] .
- Click the folder displaying your name.
- Click the Catalogs favorite.

The Catalogs page is reloaded and displayed.

You will find as time goes by that you have an extensive list of favorites, many of which you no longer need. To keep your list up to date, you can quickly delete them.

- Right-click on the Catalogs favorite and choose **D**elete from the shortcut menu.
- Click Yes .

> You can also create an Internet shortcut on your desktop by dragging a link from a page directly to the desktop. Double-clicking the desktop icon will open the browser and load the particular page.

The Catalogs favorite is deleted from the folder. Next, to delete the folder and all its contents,

- Right-click on the folder and choose **D**elete from the shortcut menu.
- Click Yes .
- Close the Favorites Explorer Bar.

> You can also delete favorites and folders using the Organize Favorites dialog box.

As a courtesy to others, delete any favorites you add to a shared computer.

Viewing the HTML Source Code

Next you want to return to The Sports Company's home page and look at the newsletter. Another way to quickly return to a page you have recently visited is to select the page from the [Back] button's drop-down menu.

> Click ⯆ next to a button to display the drop-down menu.

- Open the [Back] drop-down menu.
- Choose the Sports Company Home Page option.
- Click <u>N</u>ewsletter.

Your screen should be similar to Figure 1-14.

FIGURE 1-14

You are very pleased with how the online version of the newsletter looks. It is not in exactly the same style layout as the printed version because it was converted to a HyperText Markup Language (HTML) document.

> You will learn more about HTML in Lab 5.

Concept 7: HyperText Markup Language

All Web pages are written using a programming language called **HyperText Markup Language (HTML).** HTML commands control how the information on a page is displayed, such as font colors and size, and how an item, such as a form, will be processed. HTML also allows users to click on highlighted text or images and jump to other locations on the same page, other pages in the same site, or to other sites and locations on the Web altogether. HTML commands are interpreted by the browser software program you are using to access the WWW.

To display the HTML commands or source code for the page you are viewing,

- Choose <u>V</u>iew/Sour<u>c</u>e.
- Maximize the window.

Your screen should be similar to Figure 1-15.

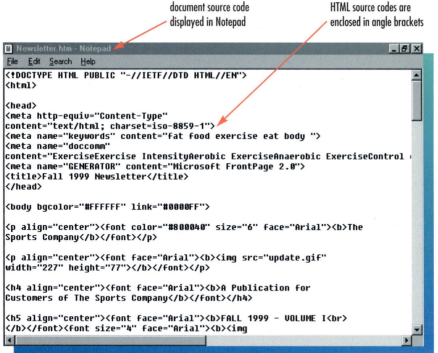

FIGURE 1-15

document source code displayed in Notepad

HTML source codes are enclosed in angle brackets

NotePad is open in a second window and displays the document source code. The source code consists of instructions enclosed in angle brackets (<>) that identify the different parts of the page and control how the text is displayed.

- Click ☒ to close the NotePad window.
- Scroll the newsletter to quickly skim the topics.

Saving Web Pages and Images

The articles in this newsletter are general in nature. The first article discusses the basics of a healthy diet, and the second the benefits of exercise. You decide you want to save a copy of the newsletter so you can read and refer to it later as you prepare your suggestions on how to improve the online newsletter.

When you click on a page, sound, or video link, the file is downloaded and temporarily stored on your computer system. Internet Explorer automatically displays the file if it is a text or HTML document, or if possible runs the appropriate software program to "play" the file for viewing or listening.

Saving a page you are viewing saves a copy of the downloaded file to your disk. Saving a link copies the file references in the link to your disk by downloading it but not displaying it. Often you may want to save page content to disk rather than read it online. This saves both online time (important when you are paying for time with a service provider) and paper. To save the current page to your data disk,

- Choose File/Save As.

The Save HTML Document dialog box on your screen should be similar to Figure 1-16.

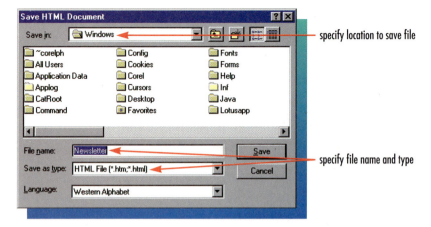

FIGURE 1-16

In this dialog box you specify the location to save the file and the file name and type. You can save the page as a plain text file (.txt) or an HTML file. A plain text file does not retain any of the original page's formatting. You can open and modify a text file with any word processor. You can also view, but not modify, a text file using Internet Explorer's **F**ile/**O**pen command. Saving the page in HTML file format saves all the formatting of the original page, which then can be viewed using the browser (offline).

- Insert a floppy disk into the appropriate drive.
- Specify the drive containing your data disk as the location.
- Change the file type to Text file [*.txt].
- Click Save.

> If you do not want to display the page to save, you can point to the link and choose Save Target **A**s from the shortcut menu.

The file is saved to your data disk and can be viewed using any word processor program. It will not include the formatting or images.

You can also save just the images from pages. Images are commonly saved as .gif or .jpg file types that can be opened and viewed using graphics programs such as Paint or a browser. You could also use any Windows word processor to view images of this type. You decide to save the image of the food guide pyramid to your data disk.

- Right-click the image of the food guide pyramid and choose **S**ave Picture As from the shortcut menu.
- If necessary, specify your data disk as the location to save the file.
- Click Save.

You can also highlight and copy selected page content to the Clipboard and then paste it into any word processor file. When copying and saving information from a Web page, be aware of the copyright protection associated with the page. This information is usually displayed at the bottom of the page. You may need the author's permission if you plan to use the information commercially; otherwise cite appropriately by giving credit as in a footnote of a research paper.

- Return to the Sports Company home page.

Using Forms

The last feature you want to check out is the feedback form. The Sports Company's home page includes an animated image of an envelope along the left side of the page. Clicking the image will open a **form** in which you complete and then submit your information.

- Click the Feedback mail icon.

Your screen should be similar to Figure 1-17.

> You may need to scroll the page to see the Feedback mail icon.

FIGURE 1-17

Forms typically include fields in which you type information, check boxes, radio buttons, pop-up menus, selection lists, and buttons for sending and clearing the information you enter. Once you complete the form, you click the button to send the form's content to the recipient. It is not necessary to address the form, as it is automatically included in the form design.

> A form's content is sent to the recipient using e-mail. You will learn about e-mail in Lab 3.

- Complete the requested information in the form.
- Click Submit Form.

Internet Explorer displays a Security Alert warning box advising you that the information you are sending may not be secure. This means it could be intercepted and used by an unintended recipient.

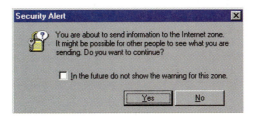

Concept 8: Security

Security is low on transmissions of information over the Internet. This is because as your message travels to the recipient, it is temporarily stored on many computers en route, making your message available to be read by others. The three most common types of security invasions are **eavesdropping,** in which a third party listens in on a private conversation, **manipulation,** in which the message is intercepted and changed, and **impersonation,** where a sender or receiver uses a false identity for communication.

As the Internet has developed, it is being used more and more for commercial purposes, so that security considerations have become extremely important. To reassure customers that the information they submit, such as credit card numbers and address information, is safe, browser software programs have made available to Web servers sophisticated methods to secure transmissions. These include the use of certificates, encryption, decryption, and digital signatures. Sites that use these features are called "secure" sites.

A **certificate** is a tamper-resistant file that identifies the individual to whom it is issued. It is issued by a certificate signer, a company that verifies and authorizes certificate requests. The certificate includes the tools, called public and private keys, needed to create a secure communication. A **public key** is the **encryption** code that is used to scramble the information in an outgoing message so that no one else can read it. A **private key** is a **decryption** code that is used to unscramble the message that was encrypted with the public key. The private key can only be used to decrypt messages that were created using the public key. The public key can be sent to anyone you want and is included with your digital signature. The recipient stores your public key and can use it to encrypt and send information to you. Without a certificate, the server can only operate insecurely.

When added to a message, a **digital signature** assures that the message was actually sent by the sender, not from an impersonator. The signature is checked by the recipient's software. Because anyone can send an encrypted message using another person's public key, they can just as easily say they are the sender. But only the sender can digitally sign a message that can be verified by anyone who has their public key.

A second type of security issue concerns files and programs that you may download from Web sites to your computer. To help minimize the risk of downloading programs that may damage your computer and the information stored in it, Internet Explorer allows you to assign Web sites to four different security zones based on how trustworthy you feel the site is. Each security zone has different security levels that determine how Internet Explorer will respond to files and programs you download from a site that you have assigned to a zone. A high security level will prevent you from downloading a file from a site, a medium security level will display a warning, and a low security level will accept the program without a warning. The default security zone is the Internet zone. Any sites that are not assigned to another zone or files that do not originate from your computer or an intranet are automatically included in this zone. It has a security level of Medium.

Internet Explorer displays a 🔒 on the status bar when you are viewing a page from a secure site.

Currently certificates are issued to organizations running servers and are not issued to Internet Explorer users.

A URL that begins with https: (instead of http:) indicates that a page comes from a server with encryption features.

Use View/**I**nternet Options/Security to establish security zones.

Printing Web Pages **IE35**

- Click 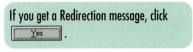.

Your screen should be similar to Figure 1-18.

> If you get a Redirection message, click Yes.

FIGURE 1-18

A confirmation message is displayed indicating the feedback form was received.

Printing Web Pages

It is also convenient to simply print the contents of the current page. For example, if you have completed a form to order an item, you may want to have a printed copy as your confirmation of your order.

- Click Back to display the Feedback Form page again.
- Choose File/Print.

The Print dialog box on your screen should be similar to Figure 1-19.

- Select the appropriate printer for your system from the Printer Name drop-down list box.

FIGURE 1-19

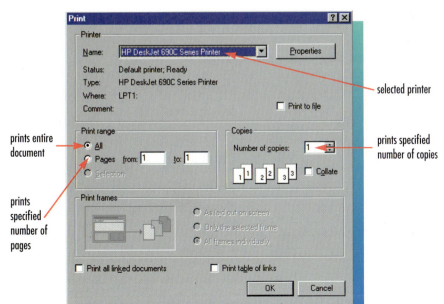

- selected printer
- prints entire document
- prints specified number of pages
- prints specified number of copies

> If a page is divided into frames, the Print Frames options in the dialog box becomes available and the currently selected frame is printed.

INTERNET EXPLORER 4

> Clicking [Print] on the Standard Buttons toolbar immediately prints the page using the default printer settings.
>
> The menu equivalent is **F**ile/**C**lose.

- Click [OK].

To exit the Internet Explorer program,

- Click [X].
- If necessary, disconnect from the Internet.

LAB REVIEW

Key Terms

alias   (IE17)
browser   (IE9)
cache   (IE24)
certificate   (IE34)
decryption   (IE34)
digital signature   (IE34)
eavesdrop   (IE34)
encryption   (IE34)
favorite   (IE26)
followed link   (IE20)
form   (IE33)
frame   (IE21)

frame set   (IE21)
History list   (IE23)
home page   (IE11)
hyperlink   (IE18)
hypertext link   (IE18)
HyperText Markup Language
   (HTML)   (IE30)
impersonation   (IE34)
inline image   (IE22)
link   (IE18)
main window   (IE10)
manipulation   (IE34)

private key   (IE34)
public key   (IE34)
security   (IE34)
server   (IE11)
startup home page   (IE11)
thumbnail   (IE22)
unfollowed link   (IE20)
Uniform Resource Locator
   (URL)   (IE15)
Web page   (IE11)
Web site   (IE11)

Command Summary

Command	Shortcut Key	Button	Action
File/**O**pen	Ctrl + O		Opens a Web page
File/Save **A**s			Saves current page to disk
File/**P**rint		[Print]	Prints current page or frame
File/**C**lose		[X]	Exits Internet Explorer
View/**T**oolbars			Hides or displays selected toolbar
View/**T**oolbars/**T**ext Labels			Hides or displays labels on Standard Buttons toolbar
View/**E**xplorer Bar/**F**avorites		[Favorites]	Displays Favorites bar

Lab Review   IE37

Command	Shortcut Key	Button	Action
View/**E**xplorer Bar/**H**istory		History	Displays History Bar
View/Sto**p**	Esc	Stop	Stops loading of a page
View/**R**efresh	F5	Refresh	Reloads current page
View/Sour**c**e			Displays HTML code for current page
View/**F**ull Screen		Fullscreen	Switches between normal view and full screen view
View/Internet **O**ptions/General/**S**ettings			Changes settings associated with cache
View/Internet **O**ptions/Security			Changes security settings
View/Internet **O**ptions/ Advanced/Multimedia/Show Pictures			Turns on and off display of inline image
Go/**B**ack	Alt + ←	Back	Displays last viewed page
Go/**F**orward	Alt + →	Forward	Displays next viewed page after using ⬛
Go/**H**ome Page		Home	Displays startup home page
Favorites/**A**dd to Favorites			Saves URL of current page
Favorites/**O**rganize Favorites			Organizes Favorites list

Matching

1. Match the following with their definition or function.

   1. [Stop]
   2. HTML
   3. home page
   4. encryption
   5. [Refresh]
   6. [Home]
   7. browser
   8. URL
   9. hypertext link
   10. favorite

   ___6___ a. displays the startup home page
   _____ b. Internet Explorer component used to browse the WWW
   ___3___ c. a connection to another Web page or location on the current page
   ___2___ d. programming language used to create Web pages
   _____ e. terminates transmission of a page
   _____ f. the scrambling of outgoing information
   _____ g. WWW address
   ___9___ h. retrieves page again from server
   _____ i. saved link to a Web page
   _____ j. opening page of a Web site

Fill-In Questions

1. Complete the following statements by filling in the blanks with the correct terms.

   a. A text file that contains links to other Web pages and graphics is called a(n) _____.

INTERNET EXPLORER 4

IE38   Navigating the Web

b. The _____ is the first page of information for a Web site.

c. The _____ is the address for the Web page.

d. A(n) _____ determines the level of trust you have assigned a Web site.

e. A connection to another Web page or another location on the current page is indicated by a(n) _____.

f. _____ images are part of a page, because they load automatically as part of the page.

g. _____ divide the Web browser's display into separate windows.

h. A(n) _____ temporarily saves page information on your computer.

i. A(n) _____ permanently stores the URL so that you can return to it at any time.

j. The _____ programming language controls how information is displayed on a Web page.

2. In the following Internet Explorer screen, letters identify important elements. Enter the correct term for each screen element in the space provided.

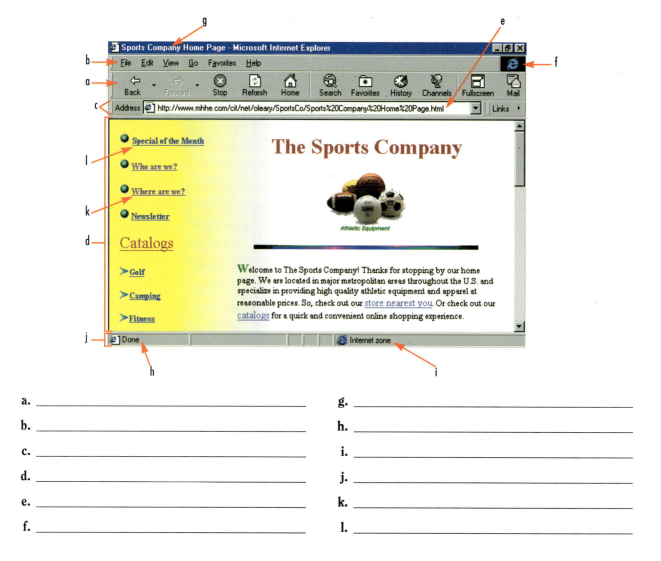

a. _____   g. _____
b. _____   h. _____
c. _____   i. _____
d. _____   j. _____
e. _____   k. _____
f. _____   l. _____

Discussion Questions

1. What is a hypertext document?
2. Explain how a message can be made secure.
3. How are the hypertext links identified?
4. What is a URL? Explain the parts of a URL.
5. Discuss the difference between history lists and favorites.

Hands-On Practice Exercises

Step by Step

Rating System
★ Easy
★★ Moderate
★★★ Difficult

1. In this problem you will learn about the Internet Explorer Help system. Internet Explorer has a detailed Help system similar to Help systems in other Windows applications.

   a. Start Internet Explorer. Choose **H**elp/**C**ontents and Index from the Internet Explorer Menu.

      The help system is divided into three areas: Contents, Index, and Search.

   b. Click the Contents tab to open the contents listing.

   c. Selecting a topic in the left frame displays the topic description in the right frame. Read the "Introducing the Web browser" topic description, then click the topic "Getting started with the Web Browser" and read the description.

   d. Click the Search tab. In the Type in the Keyword to Find text box, type: **New features.** Click the topic "What's new in Internet Explorer." Read the information on this topic.

   e. Next locate information on adding favorites. Read the information on this topic. What are the steps for adding a favorite?

   f. Close the Help window. *print*

2. In this problem you will continue to explore The Sports Company's Web site.

   a. Start Internet Explorer.

   b. Enter the URL http://www.mhhe.com/sportsco in the Address box.

   c. Click the Where Are We link. What is the address of the store in Tempe, AZ?

   d. Display the Golf Gear catalog page. Follow the Golf Bag link and display the image full size.

   e. Save the Golf Bag page to your data disk as a plain text file. Save the golf bag image to your data disk.

   f. You decide to order the aerobic stepper. Locate this item and complete steps 1 and 3 of the order form. Print this page.

   g. Return to the site's home page.

   h. Exit Internet Explorer.

   i. Using any word processor program, open the text file of the Golf Bag page you saved to your data disk. Add your name and the current date to the top of the file and print it.

   j. Using any word processor program, open the text file of the newsletter you saved to your data disk during the lab. Add your name and the current date to the top of the file. Print the file.

k. Using a graphics program such as Paint, open the image file you saved of the food guide pyramid during the lab, or insert it into a word processor file. Print the image. In the same manner, print the golf bag image file you saved.

l. Exit all programs, saving any changes you made to the files.

3. In this problem you will practice navigating the WWW by exploring your school's Web site.

   a. Start Internet Explorer. If your startup home page is not your school's Web site, enter the URL of your school's home page.

   b. Select links on your school Web site. Try to locate some of the following information. Note: If your school does not have a site set up, use the site at Arizona State University (www.asu.edu/asuweb).

      • Department you are majoring in
      • On-campus activities
      • Sporting events
      • Biographical information about your instructor
      • Admissions
      • Calendar of events

   c. Save one of the pages to your data disk as a plain text file.

   d. Print another page.

   e. Return to the site's home page.

   f. Exit Internet Explorer.

   g. Using any word processor program, open the text file of the page you saved to your data disk. Add your name and the current date to the top of the file and print it.

   h. Exit the word processor program, saving changes you made to the file.

4. One of the most popular comic strips is Dilbert. Like many other comic strips, Dilbert has its own Web site.

   a. Start Internet Explorer.

   b. Enter the address http://www.unitedmedia.com/comics/dilbert/.

   c. Explore the site and find the answers to the following questions.

      1) What are the names of the two main characters?
      2) Who is the creator of Dilbert?
      3) What is Dogbert's New Ruling Class (DNRC)?

   d. Read the most recent newsletter.

   e. Print the most recent Sunday strip.

   f. Return to the site's home page.

   g. Exit Internet Explorer.

5. You are planning a trip to the Grand Canyon and want to find out information about the park.

   a. Start Internet Explorer.

   b. Enter the address http://www.kaibab.org/.

   c. Go on a virtual visit of the Grand Canyon. When you finish, return to the home page.

   d. Select the appropriate screen resolution for your system with frames to view this site.

   e. Explore the site and find the answers to the following questions.

      1) What are three animals you might see while visiting the park?
      2) What hours is the Visitor Center open?
      3) What is the top layer of the Grand Canyon called?
      4) What river runs through the Grand Canyon?

   f. Find out what the current weather conditions are at the Grand Canyon through the University of Michigan weather center. Print this frame.

   g. Return to your startup home page.

   h. Exit Internet Explorer.

On Your Own

6. Another popular WWW site is TVNet. It is home to information about television networks and stations, and displays the current day's program listings and pointers to TV information across the Internet. TVNet's Ultimate TV List is an organized list of Internet resources on TV shows, guiding you to information and discussions about shows. See what you can find when you use the address http://www.tvnet.com/TVnet.html. Go to the Ultimate TV Show list page and enter the name of your favorite TV show in the text box. Go to the official home page for that show. Find out information about the show's lead actor and print the page.

7. Finding out the current news is another very popular service available on the Web. Sources include newspapers, wire services, and radio and television news programs. Use the following URLs to catch up on current news stories. Save two pages from different sources as plain text files. Open the text files using any word processor, add your name and the current date to the documents, and print them.

8. Use Help to find out more about security features. Discuss the Profile Assistant and the Content Advisor. Click the Product News button in the Links toolbar. Click the link to the page to learn about Internet Explorer security features and updates. Explore this page. To learn more about security, take the Security Quiz. What is Authenticode? What did you learn about cookies?

URL/Newspaper/Magazine

http://www.nytimes.com
   New York Times

http://www1.trib.com/NEWS
   List of links to U.S. and international newspapers and newswires on the Internet

http://www.sjmercury.com
   San Jose Mercury News (California)

http://www.telegraph.co.uk
   The London Telegraph's Electronic Telegraph (United Kingdom)

http://w3.one.net/~rhill/magss.html
   Time, *People*, and *PC Magazine*

http://www.usatoday.com
   USA Today

9. Everywhere you look you see references to WWW pages. Write down several URLs from articles in your local newspaper or that you see on TV. Use Internet Explorer to visit and explore these sites. Save two pages of interest to your data disk in plain text format. Save a picture image from each page to your data disk. Open the text file using any word processor and add your name and the current date to the top of the page. Print the text file. Open the picture image and print it.

10. Select several sites described on the following page and use the URLs provided to explore the sites. Save two pages of interest to your data disk in plain text format. Open the text file using any word processor and add your name and the current date to the top of the page. Print the text file. *print*

Topic	Address	Description
Boston	http://www.bostonusa.com/index.shtml	Over 1000 points of interest, event listings and descriptions, and information on Boston.
California	http://gocalif.ca.gov	California's official source of travel and tourism information.
China	http://www.ihep.ac.cn/tour/bj.html	Tour of Beijing China.
Computer games	http://www.gamesdomain.com	The Games Domain is the place to go for information on dozens of computer games. Resources include hints for specific games and an online game magazine.
Congress	http://www.lcv.org	See how your local congressperson is ranked by the League of Conservation Voters.
Congressional bills	http://thomas.loc.gov	The Library of Congress's Thomas (as in Thomas Jefferson) service lets you look up pending bills by keyword and read the Congressional Record (back to 1993).
Dinosaurs	http://pubs.usgs.gov/gip/dinosaurs	The Dinosaur fact and fiction site provides answers to some of your dinosaur questions.
Disney	http://www.disney.com	This is the official site for Disney.
Brewpub of the World	http://pekkel.uthscsa.edu/beer/brewpub/elsewhere/states.html	Brewpubs, microbreweries, and fine bars of the world.
Government	http://www.fedworld.gov	FedWorld is a gateway to dozens of federal information services in the U.S., some free, some requiring a fee to use.
Golf	http://www.golfdirect.com	A guide to golf real estate communities, golf resorts, golf courses, and golf schools of North America.
Legal information	http://www.law.cornell.edu/index.html	Cornell University's Legal Information Institute provides a variety of law-related documents, including information on specific legal issues and copies of U.S. Supreme Court decisions.
Music	http://www.music.indiana.edu/music_resources	This resource at Indiana University will help you find Web sites devoted to virtually every type of music and band.
White House	http://www.whitehouse.gov	Tours and more of the White House.
Wine	http://www.ohwy.com/wa/h/hedgecel.htm	Provides information on wineries in Washington state.

Concept Summary

1. Navigating the Web

Uniform Resource Locator

A Uniform Resource Locator (URL) provides location information that is used to navigate through the Internet to access a page.

Web Page

A Web page is a is a text file that has been created using a special programming language, called HyperText Markup Language, and that contains links to other Web pages and graphics.

Hypertext Link

A hypertext link, also called a hyperlink or simply a link, is a connection to another Web page or to another location on the current page.

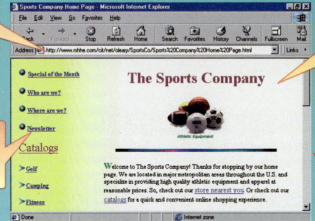

Cache

A cache is a location in your computer system that stores the page information when it is downloaded from the network.

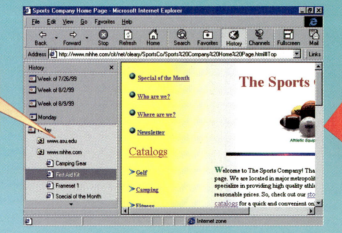

HyperText Markup Language

All Web pages are written using a programming language called HyperText Markup Language (HTML).

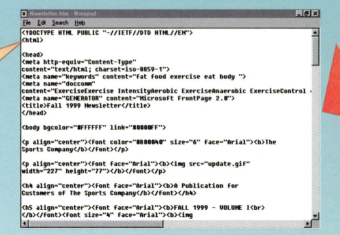

Frame

Frames divide the Web browser's display into windows. Each window is a frame that can contain a separate, scrollable page.

Concepts

- Web Page
- URL
- Hypertext Link

- Frame

- Cache

- Favorite

- HyperText Markup Language

- Security

Favorite

A favorite permanently stores the URL of a page so that you can easily access the page again by selecting the favorite from the Favorites list.

Security

Security is low on transmissions of information over the Internet. To make transmissions secure, certificates, encryption, decryption, and digital signatures are used.

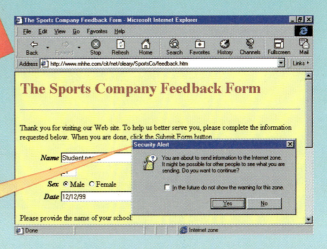

Finding Information on the Web

COMPETENCIES

After completing this lab, you will know how to:

1. Find search services.
2. Search by topic.
3. Search by keyword.
4. Conduct advanced searches.
5. Use a metasearch engine.
6. Find people and businesses.

CASE STUDY

After exploring The Sports Company's new Web site and looking at the newsletter, you feel that an additional Web page, containing links to Web sites related to the topics discussed in the newsletter, would be a worthwhile improvement to the site. The current newsletter consists of two general articles about nutrition and exercise. The plan for future newsletters is to include topics with more specific information about these two general areas. The page of related links could then be expanded and categorized as each newsletter is published.

You want to find articles on the Web that support the two general articles on nutrition and health. To locate this information, you could simply browse the Web by clicking on links from one location to another and hopefully find information related to these topics. However, this could take forever. Fortunately, many search services have been developed to help you quickly locate information on the Web. Using these tools you will see that finding this information is only a few clicks away.

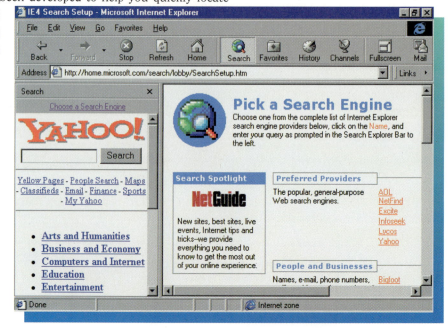

Concept Overview

The following concepts will be introduced in this lab:

1. **Search Service** — Search services are huge databases of Web pages and Internet sites that are used to locate information.
2. **Basic Search Methods** — The two basic means of searching are by navigating through topic lists or by entering a keyword or phrase into a search text box.
3. **Advanced Search Methods** — To further refine your keyword searches, you can use Boolean operators, special words that indicate a relationship among keywords in a search.
4. **Metasearch Engine** — A metasearch engine is a search utility that submits your query to several search engines simultaneously.

Finding Search Services

■ Start Internet Explorer.

To find information on the WWW, you could select hypertext links that lead you from one related topic and location to another. After many selections and possible diversions, you may finally reach your destination. If you have plenty of time and are just exploring, this is fine. But what if you want to quickly locate information about a specific topic? As the Web has grown, many Web indexing services have developed that provide search services to help you find information.

Concept 1: Search Service

Search services are huge databases of Web pages and Internet resources that are used to locate information. A search is conducted by entering keywords or by browsing topic lists. The search service generates a listing of documents that contain the keywords or that are related to the topic you have selected. In addition, some search services use a feature called concept search technology, which looks for the ideas most closely linked to the words describing what you are looking for. This increases your chances of finding what you want on the first try.

Search services can be categorized into two types: Web directories and search engines. **Web directories,** also referred to as Web Guides, are databases of Internet sites that are organized by topics or subjects. Some directories offer reviews and ratings of the sites. Most directories are also searchable, meaning you can enter a query, or a written search request, to find sites that contain the keyword you specify. Editorial staff continually add sites to the database and gladly accept suggestions from users.

Search engines also maintain huge databases of Web sites but typically offer no editorial content or categories. They use a "spider" (also called a Web crawler, robot, bot, harvester, or worm) to check out Web sites, reading and storing keywords and links and adding new sites to their existing database of sites. The spider periodically connects to servers to update its database. Different search engines use spiders that may search for different keywords in the pages. Therefore, if you conducted the same search using different search engines, the results would probably be different. Search engines typically are faster and provide a more comprehensive list of results than directories because no human intervention is needed and spiders cover much more of the Web. On the downside, typically the list is not categorized or reviewed.

(continued)

Because no one search service has all the Web pages on the Web in its index, and because the search services use different techniques and search different types of Web resources, it is advisable to use more than one engine when conducting a search. It is also helpful to know which tools may be best suited to find the type of information you need.

The following table provides a brief description of many of the most popular search services (all URLs begin with http://).

Web Directories	URL	Description
Yahoo	www.yahoo.com	Large index of hand-selected pages grouped by categories
NetGuide	www.netguide.com	Over 50,000 reviewed and categorized sites
Lycos PointCom	www.point.lycos.com	An index of top 5% of pretested and quality-checked sites in Lycos database
Lycos A2Z	www.a2z.lycos.com	Categorized directory of most popular Internet resources in Lycos database
LookSmart	www.looksmart.com	New search directory backed by Reader's Digest includes over 250,000 reviewed sites organized into 12,500 categories
Magellan	www.mckinley.com	Reviewed and rated sites; good family site
Excite	www.excite.com	Searches over 50 million indexed Web pages, or 65,000 reviewed sites. Fast, big search engine with site reviews and travel guides. Uses concept search technology and relevancy ranking.
Infoseek	www.infoseek.com	Fast, easy-to-use search engine and directory with site reviews. Contains over 50 million pages. Recommended sites are designated with a check mark.
Lycos	www.lycos.com	A large database that includes site's URL, title, and first 20 lines from which it automatically generates an abstract.
AltaVista	www.alta-vista.com	One of the largest and fastest search engines. No selection or ranking process. Generates list of pages, not sites. Best place if trying to find obscure piece of information.
AOL NetFind	www.aol.com/netfind	Uses concept search technology
WebCrawler	www.webcrawler.com	America Online's resident WWW site catalog. Small but easy to use. Includes reviewed sites.
HotBot	www.hotbot.com	Fast, though small

When looking for information on a general topic, use a directory such as Yahoo to start your search. If you are looking for a specific concept or phrase, or something that is not easily categorized, use a search engine such as AltaVista, Lycos, or Infoseek to get comprehensive listings.

There are many ways to access the different search services. The most direct method of course is to type in the URL or to select a favorite link for the search service you want to use. However, until you are familiar with the different search services and find those that you like using best, you will probably access a Web page that provides links to the search services.

Commonly, many startup home pages include a link to a page that provides a list of links to many search services. Another way is to go to a Web site that offers listings of search service resources. One resource is C/Net's search.com site (http:/www.search.com/). This site is a compilation of just about all the search services on the Web. It provides a one-stop resource to search services and even includes a description of each tool. Another is the All-in-One Search Page (http://www.albany.net/allinone), which contains a huge collection of search and reference tools. In addition, Internet Explorer provides its own page of search services and a button to quickly access it. To use this page,

- Click [Search].

> C/Net is the computer network that integrates television programming with a network of WWW sites.

> The menu equivalent is **V**iew/**E**xplorer Bar/**S**earch.

Your screen should be similar to Figure 2-1.

FIGURE 2-1

The Explorer Bar is opened and displays the Search list of basic search features for one of the available search engines. These features include a text box for entering a search keyword and a list of topics from which you can select to search by topic.

> Your Search list may display a different selected search service.

- If available, scroll the Search list to see the list of topic categories.

> Not all search services include a topic list.

The button is used to select another search service. This option will list commonly used services in a menu and an option to display a page of all available search service links on Internet Explorer's page. To see this list,

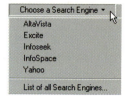

- Click .
- Choose List of All Search Engines.

Your screen should be similar to Figure 2-2.

FIGURE 2-2

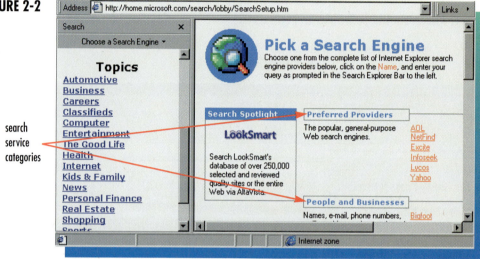

search service categories

The Pick a Search Engine page provides access to many search services categorized by the type of capabilities they provide. The Preferred Providers list contains links to the most popular search services.

> You may need to scroll the window horizontally to see the description box.

- Point to one of the links in the Preferred Providers category to see a brief description of the service in the box to the right.
- Scroll the page to see the search services in the other categories.

You decide to use Yahoo, one of the original search services developed, to help you locate information on health and nutrition.

- Click Yahoo (in the Preferred Providers category).

The Search Explorer bar now reflects the features available in Yahoo. It includes a search text box and Yahoo's top-level category listing.

You can also go directly to Yahoo's home page using Go/Search the Web.

Searching by Topic

Depending upon the type of search service you are using, there are two basic ways to find information: searching by topic or by keyword.

> ### Concept 2: Basic Search Methods
>
> The two basic means of searching are by navigating through topic lists or by entering a keyword or phrase into a search text box. Some search services offer both methods, others only one.
>
> Use the **topic search** when you are looking for general information. Using this method you navigate through a hierarchy of topic listings that group the items in the database into subject categories, such as art, business, and sports. The main subject groupings are further categorized into subtopics; for example, the sports group may have subdivisions of cycling, baseball, and soccer. As you continue to make selections from the topic groups, you narrow the number of listings that will be available to those that more precisely match the information you are seeking.
>
> If you are looking for a specific concept or a phrase, use the **keyword search** method. The search program compares this text with some part of the text it has sorted in its database—title, URL, text, a description, abstract, or review—then it displays a list of all pages in its database that contain the text you specified.
>
> Some simple tips for finding what you want using keywords:
>
> 1. Be specific. Use more descriptive, specific words as opposed to general ones. The more descriptive the keyword you enter, the better your results.
> 2. Use multiple words. You may want to use synonyms to help narrow the field of your search.
> 3. Leave out nonessential words like prepositions and articles; most search programs ignore them anyway.
>
> If the search yields too few results or "hits," your keyword may be too specific or the incorrect term. Try again using different or less specific words. Conversely, if you get too many hits, you may want to narrow the field by using more specific words.

Since the articles in the newsletter provide general information about nutrition and fitness, you want to begin by finding several sites that provide general advice on these topics, rather than information about a specific topic. To do this you will perform a topic search.

■ Click Health.

Your screen should be similar to Figure 2-3.

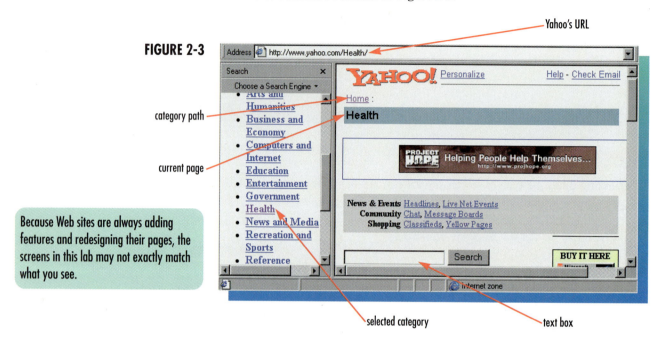

FIGURE 2-3

Because Web sites are always adding features and redesigning their pages, the screens in this lab may not exactly match what you see.

After a few moments, a page containing links to health topics is loaded in the right window. Notice from the URL that you are at Yahoo's Web site.

Note: If you receive a message indicating you cannot connect to a site, it may be that the maximum number of users is accessing the location. Resubmit your request several times and you will probably get on. If not, skip to the next section, "Searching by Keyword," on page IE55 and return to this section later.

At the top of the page is the path of category selections you have made. In this case, you started at Yahoo's home page (Home). The name of the currently displayed page, Health, is displayed in the bar below the category path. Clicking on the Home link will return you directly to Yahoo's home page.

You can also click the red Yahoo! banner at the top of every page to return to Yahoo's main page.

Below this are several links to suggested services offered by Yahoo and a search text box. Below this is another subject list.

■ Scroll the right window to see the subject list.

Your screen should be similar to Figure 2-4.

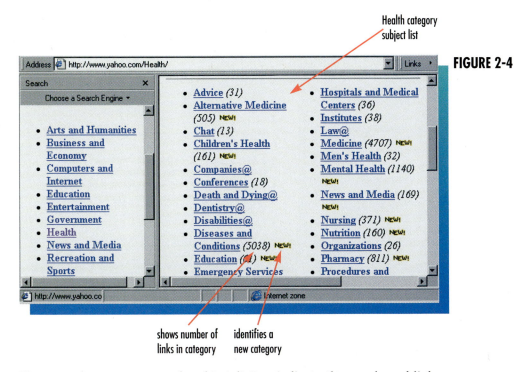

FIGURE 2-4

The parentheses next to each subject listing indicate the number of links included in that category. An @ symbol means the link goes to a different Yahoo category. New categories are also identified with the **NEW!** symbol. Links with 👓 mean these links are recommended.

Since the newsletter articles briefly discuss activities to improve fitness, you want to refer readers to Web sites on this topic. This category contains approximately 100 links (at the time of this writing) to Web pages related to Fitness.

■ Click Fitness.

This page includes another category listing as well as a listing of Web pages related to health and fitness. The path of selections you have made is extended to include your most recent selection (Home:Health:). The previously selected category is now a link back to that page.

■ Scroll the page to see the subject listing of Fitness topics, followed by a listing of links to Web pages on fitness.

Your screen should be similar to Figure 2-5.

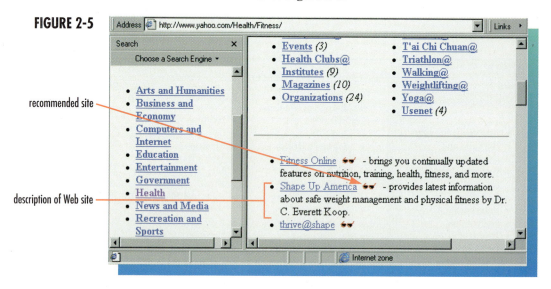

FIGURE 2-5

Your screen may display different sites as new ones are added and old ones removed.

Each item in the list consists of the page title as a hypertext link to the site and a brief description of the site. In addition, if the Yahoo staff has reviewed a site, a ▶REVIEW◀ symbol is displayed. Clicking ▶REVIEW◀ will display the review.

The description of the Shape Up America site appears to contain content similar to the articles in this month's newsletter. To check out this site,

■   Click Shape Up America.

Your screen should be similar to Figure 2-6.

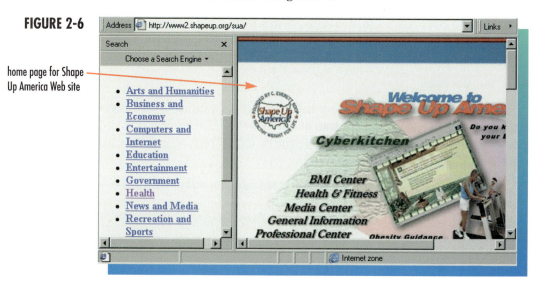

FIGURE 2-6

The Shape Up America home page is downloaded. Unfortunately, with the Explorer Bar open, the viewing space for the page content is smaller, making it necessary to scroll the window more often. To see the page better and further check out the site's content,

- Click ☒ to close the Search Explorer Bar.
- Scroll the page and click the Health & Fitness link.

This page looks interesting. It provides a link to an assessment of your fitness level as well as to basic information about fitness and different types of physical activity.

- Click the Assess Your Fitness Level link.

You think this looks like a good site for inclusion in the newsletter-related links page. As you continue your search for sites related to the newsletter articles, you want to create a list of the sites to give your supervisor. To do this you can copy the site description to a word processor document.

- Use the ⬅Back menu to return to the Yahoo Health:Fitness page of topics.
- Select the Yahoo Shape Up America site description.
- Copy the selection to the Clipboard (**E**dit/**C**opy or Ctrl + C).
- Open WordPad and click to paste the selection into a new document.

Your screen should be similar to Figure 2-7.

> To highlight the description, drag when the mouse pointer is an I-beam.

> Use 🏁Start/**P**rograms/Accessories to load WordPad.

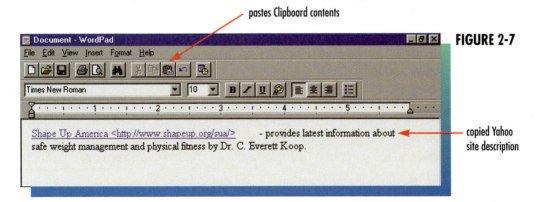

FIGURE 2-7

- Switch back to Internet Explorer and go to several other sites from the Yahoo Health:Fitness page list. When you have found another good site, copy the description to the WordPad document.

> Use the taskbar button to switch between applications.

Searching by Keyword

Next you will conduct a search by entering keywords in a search text box. The first article in the newsletter discusses the basics of eating a healthy diet. You will use the Infoseek search service to locate information on this topic.

- If necessary, switch back to Internet Explorer.
- Click 🔍Search to redisplay the Search Explorer Bar.

> You can also conduct a simple search by typing "go," "find," or "?" in the Address bar followed by the keywords and Explorer will start a search using its predetermined search service (Yahoo by default).

> Whenever the Security Alert dialog box appears as you submit a keyword, click **Yes**.

- Use the Search list to change to the Infoseek search service.
- Click in the search text box and type **diet**.
- Click **seek**.
- Scroll the Search list to see the first few links to Web pages in the result list.

Your screen should be similar to Figure 2-8.

FIGURE 2-8

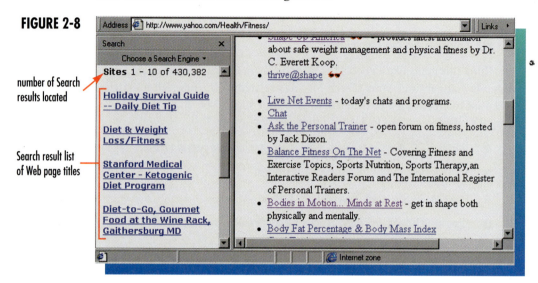

When conducting a keyword search using the Search list, the results of your search are displayed in the Search list instead of the main window area to the right. This makes it easy to quickly check out the links without losing track of the search results.

Infoseek shows how many pages it located that contain the keyword "diet" and displays the first 10 search results. To save space, the Search list displays the page titles only. If you want to know more about a site before selecting the link, you can point to it to display a site description in a screen tip.

- Display the site descriptions for several sites in the list.

The site description consists of a brief summary of the site, a relevancy percentage, the URL of the Web page, and the size of the file. The relevancy percent value indicates how relevant the site is to your keyword search. A site gets a higher percentage rating if the keyword is found in the title or near the start of the document. It also gets a higher rating if the number of times the keyword is found in the document is more than others and if the document contains a keyword that is relatively uncommon in the database. The highest rated sites are listed first.

Searching by Keyword **IE57**

- Click the next 10 link at the bottom of the search result list to see the next 10 search results.
- Scroll the list of results and click prev 10 to return to the previous page of results.

After quickly checking out the first two pages of search results, you see that the sites mostly link to pages about weight loss and diet products rather than to information about nutrition. You decide to change the search keyword to locate information on nutrition. Notice that Infoseek has a Search text box at the top of each page in which you can specify a new search or refine your current search by restricting the new search to the located documents.

- Type **nutrition information** in the Search text box.
- Select the Search These Results option.
- Click seek .
- Scroll the Search list to see the beginning of the search result list.

This option may also appear as "Search only within."

Your screen should be similar to Figure 2-9.

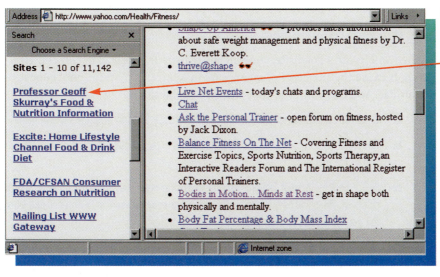

FIGURE 2-9

results containing both keywords appear at the top of the result list

When you enter multiple words, Infoseek displays Web pages containing all the words in your query at the top of the result list. This feature broadens your search, much as if you had navigated through the topic list, but a lot faster. Generally, the longer the keyword query, the better the results. If you know the specific type of information you are looking for, it is more efficient to use a keyword search rather than a topic search.

These search results appear to provide information more related to the topics discussed in the newsletter.

- Click on a link of your choice. *print number (1) one write your name and one too.*

INTERNET EXPLORER 4

Your screen should be similar to Figure 2-10.

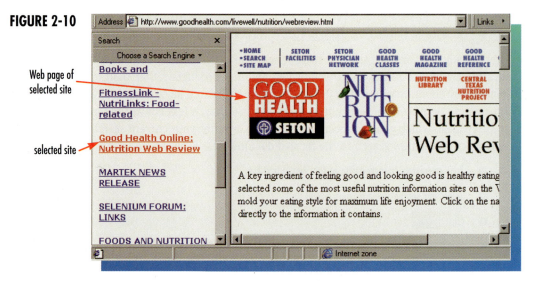

FIGURE 2-10

The right window displays the Web page you selected.

- Explore this site and several others from the result list.

When you locate a good site, you will add it to your WordPad document. However, because the site description appears in a screen tip, you cannot copy it to WordPad. You can, however, copy the URL to the site.

- Right-click on an appropriate site title and select Copy Shortcut from the shortcut menu.

- Paste the shortcut in the WordPad document and enter the page title and a brief description of the site.

- Switch back to Internet Explorer and go to several other sites from the Infoseek search result list. When you have found another good site, copy the shortcut to WordPad and enter the page title and site description.

- Close the Explorer Bar.

Advanced Searches

As you can see, when conducting a keyword search, you can get search results that more closely match your needs by entering a more specific keyword or by using several related keywords. In addition, you can use advanced search methods.

Concept 3: Advanced Search Methods

To further refine your keyword searches, you can use **Boolean operators,** special words that indicate a relationship among keywords in a search. The most common Boolean operators are AND, OR, and NOT. These operators must appear in ALL CAPS and with a space on each side in order to work. They allow you to combine keywords to include the information you want and to eliminate other information. The Boolean operators as well as several other commonly used advanced search features and their effects are described in the table below.

Operator	Effect
AND (or &)	Documents found must contain all words joined by the word AND. The AND operator is assumed by many search services. Example: *rock AND roll AND music* finds articles on rock and roll music.
+ (plus sign)	Specifies that each word preceded with a + must appear in the search results. Example: *+rock +roll +music* finds articles with all three words, whereas *rock +roll +music* will include roll and music, but not necessarily rock.
OR (or |)	Documents must contain at least one of the words connected by OR. Example: *rock OR roll* finds documents containing the word rock or roll (or in some cases, both).
− (minus sign)	Specifies that words preceded with a − cannot appear in the search results. Example: *+billiards −equipment −supplies* finds articles with the word billiards but not equipment or supplies.
NOT (or !)	Excludes words, but must be used with the operators AND or OR as in AND NOT or OR NOT. Example: *pets AND NOT cats,* or *pets !cats,* finds articles about pets excluding cats.
Near (or ~)	Specifies two words that must appear close together on a page. Example: *wolves~domesticated* finds articles on wolves that have been domesticated.
( )	Used to group portions of Boolean queries together for more complicated finds. Example: *pets AND (cats OR birds)* finds pages with the word pets and either the word cats or birds.
" (quotation marks)	Finds only exact multiple-word phrases, whereas not using quotes finds documents containing any of those words, in any order. Example: *"Air Force 1"* finds only documents with this exact phrase.
* (wildcard)	Indicates any amount of letters or symbols. Example: *air** finds pages that contain words like airmail, airplane, airport, and airspeed.

(continued)

IE60 Finding Information on the Web

Some other ways to make your searches more accurate are:

- Limit the scope of the search by specifying an area of the database to search, such as a topic category, newsgroups, e-mail, or mailing lists.
- Use a search feature that looks for whole words only or pieces of the words.
- Use a search feature to find all keywords with or without regard to case.
- Some search services include a "more like this" link next to the result article link. Clicking this link instructs the search engine to use that document as an example of what else to look for, to find more sites similar to the one you liked.
- Another search service feature you may see allows you to enter a revised keyword query that will expand or narrow your search results. Look for a Refine Your Find or Search These Results link.

Because the advanced search features vary with the search service you are using, it is a good idea to check out each search service's page of information on conducting advanced searches and tips. This will explain its particular features and give you more control over how the search is conducted.

Next you want to find information specifically about the food guide pyramid that is discussed in the newsletter article. You will use the Excite search service to locate this information using some advanced search features. Another way to access a search site is to go directly to the site by typing the URL in the Address bar. To go to the Excite search engine site,

- Type **excite** in the Address bar.
- Type **pyramid** in the Search text box.
- Click Search.
- Scroll the page to see the first few search results.

Your screen should be similar to Figure 2-11.

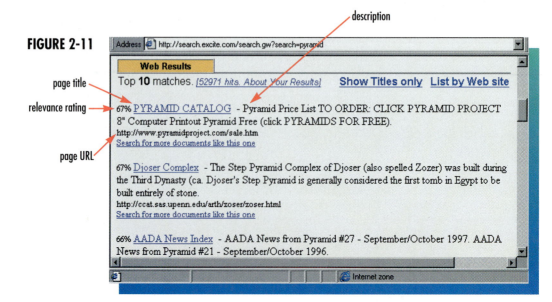

FIGURE 2-11

Excite also lists 10 search results at a time on a page. Each result includes a relevance rating (%), the title, URL, and a brief summary of the content. The most relevant documents are listed first.

Notice that many of the results do not have anything to do with food or nutrition guidelines. This is because all sites that contain the word "pyramid" are listed. This includes sites that sell pyramid-shaped pet houses, Egyptian pyramids, and so on. To make the search more accurate, you will modify the search query to include the word "food" and exclude the word "Egypt."

- Display the Search text box.

In addition to a Search box at the top and bottom of each page, Excite also includes a list of related words. You can click on a word to add it to your search query to help you identify exactly what it is about the particular topic that you are interested in locating. In this case, however, none of the words are appropriate. To refine your search,

> Many search services include a feature that allows you to select advanced search options from list boxes rather than to have to type the sequence in the correct format in the Search text box. Excite's is accessed using the Power Search link.

- Edit the keyword search to **+pyramid +food -egypt**.
- Click **Search Again**.
- Scroll the page to see the search results.

Your screen should be similar to Figure 2-12.

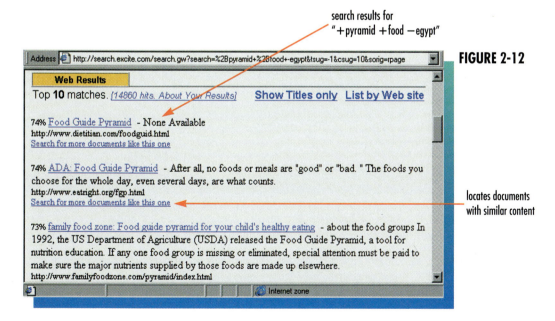

FIGURE 2-12

Now only sites that include the word "pyramid" or "food" but not "Egypt" are included in the search results. Also notice that Excite includes a link to search for similar documents with each result. This feature instructs the search engine to use the content of that document as an example in a new search to find more sites similar to the one you liked.

- Click the Search for more documents like this one link of any search result that refers to the food guide pyramid.
- Scroll the list of related sites.

The results much more closely match the type of information you need. Perhaps the most effective search would have been to enter the phrase "food guide pyramid" in quotes as the search query. To see what the results would be using this phrase,

- Enter **"food guide pyramid"** in the Search text box.
- Click Search Again.
- Scroll the page to see the first few listed results.

Your screen should be similar to Figure 2-13.

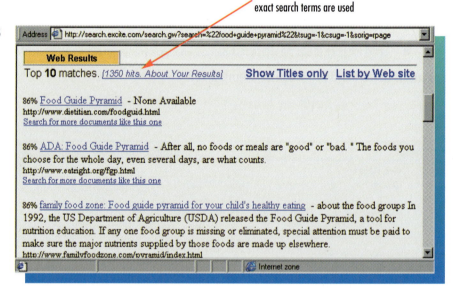

FIGURE 2-13

fewer hits result when more exact search terms are used

All the sites included in the results contain the exact phrase you specified, resulting in fewer hits and so making the search results right on the mark.

- Explore several of the sites from the Excite search results list. When you have found another good site, copy the description to the WordPad document.
- Switch to the Internet Explorer window.

As you can see, using the advanced search features greatly helps to refine your search to locate documents that are as close as possible to the content you are seeking. Even the order you enter the words in the query has an effect on the results. If you were to perform the same search using different search services, you would see many of the same search results. But each search service will include sites that were not included by the others. For this reason, even if you find you have a favorite search service, it is advisable to check several to do a more thorough search.

Using a Metasearch Engine

As you can imagine, searching using several search engines in sequence is tedious and produces many duplicate hits. This problem has been largely overcome by the development of search utilities called metasearch engines.

> **Concept 4: Metasearch Engine**
>
> A **metasearch engine** is a search utility that submits your query to several search engines simultaneously. As with a standard search engine, you enter keywords. The list of results is usually ordered by relevance with all the duplicates removed. It then lets you repeat the search by selecting other search engines or by modifying your keyword query. The major benefit to users of metasearch engines is the increased speed of conducting and modifying searches and of scanning the search results.
>
> Many of these search utilities are available online for free. Others are utility programs that you can purchase that will conduct the same type of search as the online metasearch engines with fewer restrictions. Several of the online metasearch engines and the utility programs you can purchase are listed in the tables below.
>
> | Online Engine | URL |
> | --- | --- |
> | SavvySearch | http://guaraldi.cs.colostate.edu:2000/form |
> | SavvySearch Version 2 | http://guaraldi.cs.colostate.edu:2000/form?beta |
> | Dogpile | http://www.dogpile.com |
> | MetaCrawler | http://metacrawler.com |
> | FerretSoft's WebFerret | http://www.ferretsoft.com |
>
> | Utility Program | URL |
> | --- | --- |
> | BitSafe Computer Services Arf | http://dwave.net./~bitsafe/arf/index.html |
> | ForeFront Group's WebSeeker | http://www.ffg.com |
> | Symantec's Internet FastFind | http://www.symantec.com |
> | Quarterdeck's WebCompass | http://www.quarterdeck.com |

SavvySearch Version 2 is currently under development and offers many enhancements over the original version.

At the time of this writing, Internet Explorer's Pick a Search Engine page does not include any of the metasearch engines.

IE64 Finding Information on the Web

> The SavvySearch site is often busy, indicating that there are insufficient computing resources for the service's query load—a common problem with newly popular resources on the Internet.

- Use one of the search services to locate the SavvySearch metasearch engine, or enter the URL http://guaraldi.cs.colostate.edu:2000/form in the Address bar to go directly to the site.
- If necessary, display SavvySearch's Search Form.

Your screen should be similar to Figure 2-14.

FIGURE 2-14

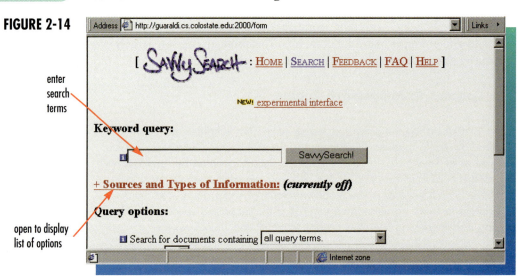

enter search terms

open to display list of options

> If you are using SavvySearch Version 2, the listing of Sources and Types of Information appears immediately below the Search text box rather than as a link.

You will use SavvySearch to search for information on the benefits of exercise as discussed in the second newsletter article. Below the text box are the search option settings.

- If necessary, click Sources and Types of Information to display the list of options.
- Type **exercise "weight loss"** in the Search text box.
- Scroll the page to see the list of sources and options.

Your screen should be similar to Figure 2-15.

FIGURE 2-15

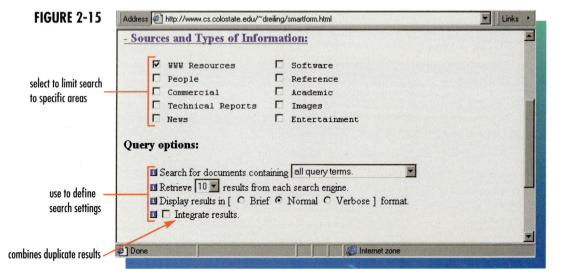

select to limit search to specific areas

use to define search settings

combines duplicate results

The Sources and Types of Information link opens a list of categories you can select to limit your search to specific areas of the Internet. The WWW Resources option is selected by default. The three query options can be used to refine the search. By default they are set to require that all search terms are included in the search result documents, to display 10 hits from each search engine, and to display a normal amount of description.

- To start the search using the default search settings, click SavvySearch! .
- Scroll the results list to the bottom of the page.

Your screen should be similar to Figure 2-16.

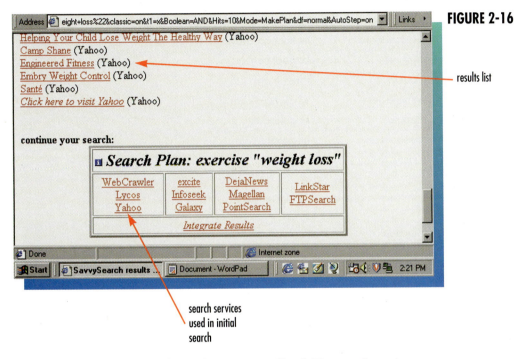

FIGURE 2-16

results list

search services used in initial search

The search results from three search services are listed. The search services are selected based on an analysis of such factors as the content of the submitted query and the current response times of the search services. At the bottom of the page is the table that displays the services in groups of three. The first group contains the three services that SavvySearch felt were most likely to produce the results you wanted and were used to conduct the initial search. You can select a different group of search services on which to run your search by clicking the appropriate cell of the table.

- Select links to several of the search results listed.
- Add a description and the URL of two of these sites to the WordPad document.
- Enter your name and the current date at the top of the WordPad document. Save the WordPad document to your data disk as Newsletter Links. Print the document. Close the file and exit WordPad.

Print #3

Finding People and Businesses

> You will learn about e-mail addresses in Lab 3.

Another source of information are databases, commonly called the **white** and **yellow pages,** that are used to search for people or businesses. It used to be that the only way to locate people and businesses was through the traditional printed white and yellow pages and through telephone directory assistance. Now these same services and more are offered by online search services. Many of these services also provide phone and mail address information, in addition to e-mail addresses. Some of these services are listed in the table below.

> The URL begins with http://www unless indicated otherwise.

White Pages	URL Description
Switchboard	switchboard.com
BigFoot	bigfoot.com
Four11	four11.com
WhoWhere	whowhere.com
Populus	populus.net
InfoSpace	infospace.com

Yellow Pages	URL Description
Big Book	bigbook.com
US West Dex	yp.uswest.com
GTE SuperPages(sm)	superpages.com
Switchboard	switchboard.com
InfoSpace	infospace.com

To quickly locate many of these sites,

- Click [Search].

- Choose List of all Search Engines from the Choose a Search Engine drop-down list.

The People and Businesses section of the Pick a Search Engine page contains links to white pages indexes. You will use the InfoSpace white pages site to search for a person's e-mail address by entering the requested information in the search text boxes.

> You can also type InfoSpace in the Address bar to access this site.

- Click InfoSpace.

Your screen should be similar to Figure 2-17.

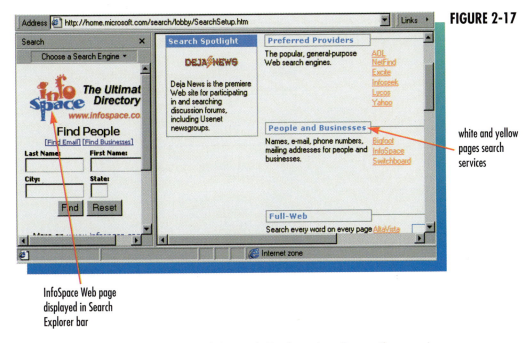

FIGURE 2-17

white and yellow pages search services

InfoSpace Web page displayed in Search Explorer bar

The InfoSpace page is displayed in the Search Explorer bar. To see the page in a separate window,

- Right-click the Search Explorer Bar title bar and choose **O**pen in Window from the shortcut menu.
- If necessary, maximize the new window.

A second Internet Explorer window is open and displays the InfoSpace search page. The taskbar displays two Internet Explorer buttons.

- Click Find Email.

Your screen should be similar to Figure 2-18.

FIGURE 2-18

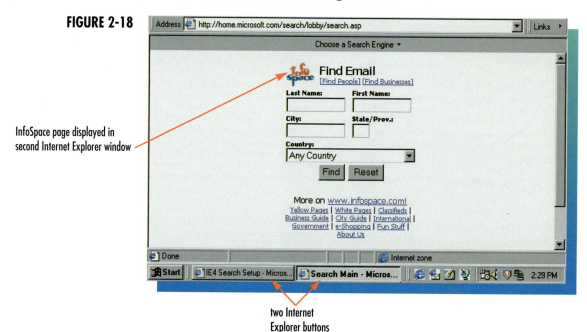

InfoSpace page displayed in second Internet Explorer window

two Internet Explorer buttons

- Enter the following information in the appropriate text boxes:

    Last name: **Brown**
    First name: leave blank
    Enter your city and state in the appropriate boxes.

- Click Find.

- Scroll the page to view the first few results.

Your screen should be similar to Figure 2-19.

FIGURE 2-19

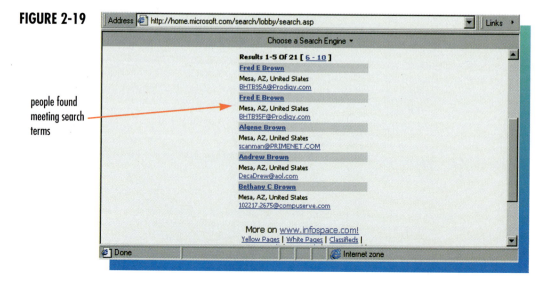

people found meeting search terms

A list of those people with last names of Brown in your city and state is displayed. Of course, the more specific you can make your search request, the fewer matches will be located.

The procedure to search using the yellow pages is much the same except that only business sites are included in the site's database.

- Continue to search for other people or businesses of your choice.
- When you are done, close both Internet Explorer windows.
- If necessary, disconnect from the Internet.

LAB REVIEW

Key Terms

Boolean operator   (IE59)
keyword search   (IE51)
metasearch engine   (IE63)

search engine   (IE47)
search service   (IE47)
topic search   (IE51)

Web directory   (IE47)
white pages   (IE66)
yellow pages   (IE66)

Command Summary

Command	Button	Action
View/**E**xplorer Bar/**S**earch		Opens Search Explorer bar
Go/**S**earch the Web		Opens Search Web page

Matching

1. Match the following with their definition or function.

1) keyword   ____   a. Boolean operator to find all words joined by the operator

2) Yahoo   ____   b. word used to locate pages that contain specific information

3) Web directory   ____   c. search utility that submits query to several search engines

4) AND   ____   d. databases of Internet sites that can be searched by topic

5) search engine   ____   e. database of categorized sites that are compiled by people

6) AltaVista   ____   f. Boolean operator to find one of the words joined by the operator

7) yellow pages   ____   g. uses a spider to locate Web sites

8) OR   ____   h. database that contains people's phone numbers and e-mail addresses

9) metasearch   ____   i. index of hand-selected pages grouped by category

10) white pages   ____   j. database that contains business phone numbers and e-mail addresses

IE70 Finding Information on the Web

Fill-In Question

1. In the following Internet Explorer screen, letters identify important elements. Enter the correct term for each screen element in the space provided.

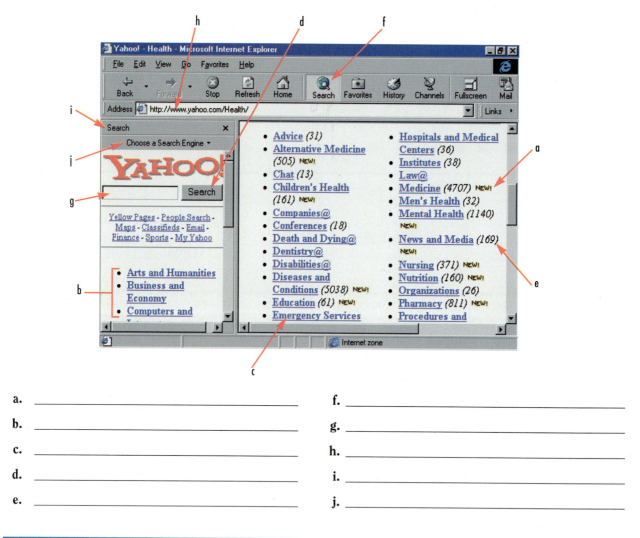

a. _____   f. _____
b. _____   g. _____
c. _____   h. _____
d. _____   i. _____
e. _____   j. _____

Discussion Questions

1. Describe the two types of search services. Explain why you would want to use more than one search service to locate information.
2. Discuss three basic procedures you can use to make your keyword searches more effective.
3. Discuss five advanced search procedures.
4. How can you find someone's e-mail address?

Hands-On Practice Exercises

Step by Step

1. You want to see if you can find information about the town you live in on the WWW.

   a. Open the Internet Explorer Search bar.
   b. Using three different search engines, search for information on the town or city you live in (or close by).
   a. Note what pages and the types of information each search engine locates.
   c. Narrow your search by adding keywords to eliminate sites you do not want to find.
   d. In WordPad or any other word processor, list the three search engines you used and the types of pages found. What words did you add to narrow your search? *print the home page.*

2. One of the best uses of the WWW is to display graphic images. An excellent example of this can be found at the WebMuseum, a database of images and information about famous artists. The WebMuseum consists of two parts: an exhibit of art and a tour of Paris.

   a. Using a search service of your choice, locate the WebMuseum.
   b. Follow the directions on the Welcome page to select a WebMuseum site that is close to your location.
   c. Go to the Famous Paintings exhibition.
   d. Select an art category of your choice (such as Impressionism) from the Themes Index.
   e. Read a biography of one of the artists.
   f. Save the biography and an image of your choice by that artist to your data disk.
   g. Return to the site's home page and take a tour of Paris.
   h. Open the biography in a word processor and add your name and date to the top of the file.
   i. Print the biography and the picture.

3. In this problem you will use another white pages search service to locate e-mail addresses.

   a. Using the Four11 white pages (www.four11.com), search for your name. Did you find yourself?
   b. If you found yourself, you have registered previously for this service. If you did not find yourself, click Add Me. Follow the directions on the screen to add your name and personal information to the service. As of this writing, this is a free service that will help friends and family locate your e-mail address.
   c. Use the Four11 white pages to search for e-mail addresses for friends and family.

4. You are planning to rent a movie at the local video store and want to check out several movie reviews on the Web before you go.

   a. Using a search service of your choice, locate a movie review for a recent movie on video. Print the review.
   b. Save the search service's description and the URL to a WordPad document.
   c. Use a different search service to locate a movie review for an old movie (more than 10 years old). Print the review.
   d. Save the search service's description and the URL to the WordPad document.

e. Perform a topic search using Yahoo to locate a Web site that reviews current movies. Print a review of a current movie.

f. Add your name and the current date to the WordPad document. Print the document.

On Your Own

5. You may need to travel at some point during your career. The Internet Travel Network lets you track fares and prices on domestic airlines. The system automatically displays the lowest available fare for an itinerary and can be used to book reservations and send tickets to the user. This is a free service but has a charge for booking tickets. Locate this service and establish an account. Check prices for a trip you would like to take. Check several airlines and find the lowest price available.

6. You are preparing a paper for a course in your field of study. Use Internet Explorer to locate three text files that contain information on the topic of your paper. Copy and paste the page title and URL to a word processor document. Include a brief summary of the information in the text files. Locate two pictures that may be useful in the paper. Save the pictures to your data disk. Add your name to the text document. Print the text file of descriptions and URLs along with the two pictures.

7. Using a search service of your choice, search on San Francisco or a city of your choice and locate information on hotel accommodations. Find pages that allow you to locate hotel rooms in the city by price, location, type of hotel, and so on. Locate photographs of hotel lobbies and rooms. If possible, find pages that allow you to check availability. After checking out three hotels, which one would you recommend staying in and why?

8. Channels are the newest edition to Internet Explorer. Use Help to find out about Channels, then search the WWW for more information about how this feature works. Using WordPad or another word processor, write a brief paper summarizing your findings.

9. How people work has changed dramatically with the introduction of computers. As a consequence, many health-related side effects such as repetitive motion injuries commonly occur. Conduct a search for information about computer-related health problems. Write a brief paper summarizing your findings. Include several suggestions on solutions. Using the information you found, analyze your workspace. What changes can you make to your workspace to make it ergonomically safe? Include the changes you made to your workspace in your report. Print the report.

Concept Summary

Finding Information on the Web

Search Service

Search services are huge databases of Web pages and Internet sites that are used to locate information.

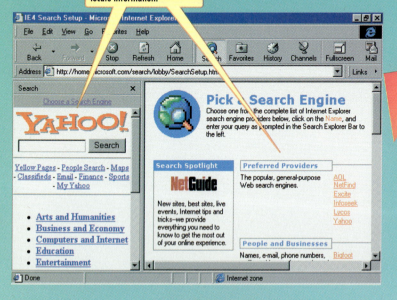

Concepts

- Search Service
- Basic Search Methods
- Advanced Search Methods
- Metasearch Engine

Metasearch Engine

A metasearch engine is a search utility that submits your query to several search engines simultaneously.

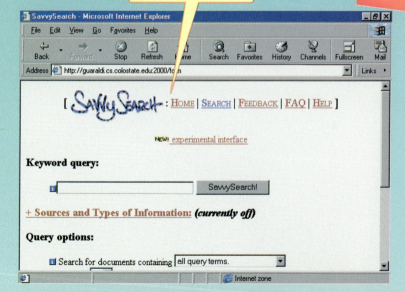

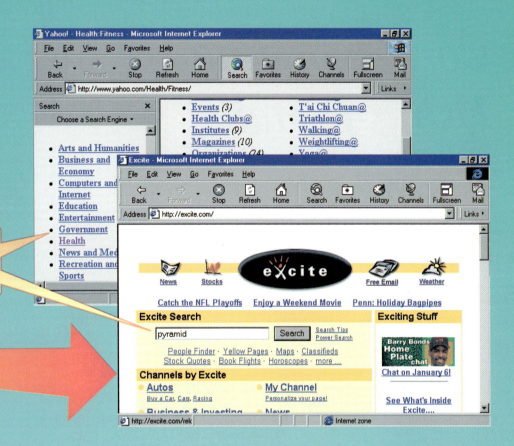

Basic Search Methods

The two basic means of searching are by navigating through topic lists or by entering a keyword or phrase into a search text box.

Advanced Search Methods

To further refine your keyword searches, you can use Boolean operators, special words that indicate a relationship among keywords in a search.

Corresponding Using E-Mail

COMPETENCIES

After completing this lab, you will know how to:

1. Set up Outlook Express.
2. Compose an e-mail message.
3. Spell-check and edit a message.
4. Format a message.
5. Attach a file.
6. Send a message.
7. Open an attachment.
8. Check incoming mail.
9. Create an address book.
10. Reply to e-mail.
11. Forward a message.
12. Save a message.
13. Delete a message.
14. Print a message.

CASE STUDY

Over the past few days, you have been looking at The Sports Company Web site and considering how changes could be made to improve the newsletter. Your main suggestion is to add a page of links to fitness and nutrition topics related to the content of the articles in the newsletter.

You decide to send an e-mail message (shown below) to the regional manager explaining your suggestion, along with a copy of the Web sites you have located that would complement the current edition of the newsletter.

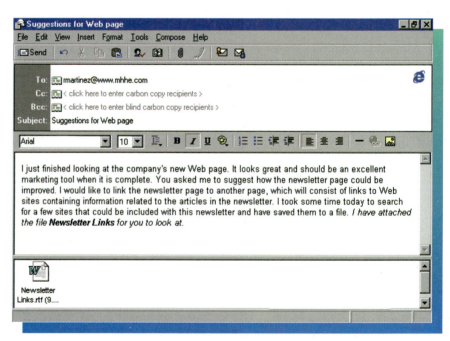

Concept Overview

The following concepts will be introduced in this lab:

1. How E-Mail Works — E-mail requires the use of two programs: a mailer program and a delivery system.

2. E-Mail Address — On the Internet, each person has a unique e-mail address or means of identification.

3. Mail Server — Two types of mail servers work together to handle incoming and outgoing e-mail messages.

4. E-Mail Folders — Outlook Express includes several folders that are used to organize and store e-mail messages.

5. Parts of an E-Mail Message — An e-mail message consists of two basic parts, the header and the body.

6. E-Mail Style and Netiquette — E-mail is a fairly new way of communicating and has developed its own style and set of rules of courteous electronic communications called Netiquette (net etiquette).

7. Address Book — Rather than trying to remember many different e-mail addresses, you can create a file of addresses called an address book.

What Is E-Mail?

The ability to communicate with others over the Internet is one of the prime reasons for its success and popularity. One of the original forms of communicating on the Internet is electronic mail or **e-mail.** E-mail allows individuals to send and receive written messages via computer.

Concept 1: How E-Mail Works

E-mail requires the use of two programs. The first is the e-mail software program, more frequently called a **mailer program** or **reader program.** The mailer program provides the means of creating, sending, and reading e-mail messages. The mailer software you will use is called Outlook Express. There are many other e-mail programs, such as Eudora, Pegasus Mail, and Microsoft Internet Mail, that perform the same function as Outlook Express. A mailer program deposits the e-mail message you send in an electronic **mailbox,** which is located on a computer called a **mail server** at a school, workplace, or Internet service provider. Each user is assigned a private mailbox when they establish an e-mail account. The mailbox is identified with the user's Internet e-mail address. You will learn about e-mail addresses shortly.

The second program is the delivery system that routes the e-mail message over the Internet to the intended recipient. As the message travels, it passes from one mail server to another until it reaches its destination, where it is placed in the recipient's mailbox.

E-mail uses **store-and-forward** technology. This means that if the recipient's computer is not available for mail delivery, the store-and-forward feature enables applications to hold messages or information for later delivery. Stored messages are then automatically forwarded when network contact is reestablished.

Corresponding Using E-Mail

> Between 1988 and 1994, the U.S. Postal Service's market share dropped from 77 to 62 percent, while electronic alternatives increased their share from 19 to 36 percent.

E-mail is the main means of communication between Internet users, with more than 3 billion e-mail messages sent over the Internet each month, a sixfold increase in two years. Today, with 60 million Americans having access to e-mail, and 12.8 million U.S. households using e-mail from home, it is the most widely used application on the Internet. It is estimated that by the year 2005, more than 5 billion personal messages will be sent each day.

One reason for e-mail's growing popularity is the change in the workplace from central offices to home or on-the-road offices. E-mail provides a convenient communications pathway to coworkers and customers and allows computer users to exchange information and data files directly with one another. Another reason is that e-mail is cost effective. For example, a message that costs $3.12 when sent by telephone, or $1.46 by fax, costs only 23 cents by e-mail. In addition to cost savings, there is a speed advantage. Messages can be transferred between countries in minutes and within the United States in seconds. On the other hand, network outages, maintenance, or repair problems may cause a message to be delayed days or even weeks. As e-mail continues to gain in popularity, the U.S. Postal Service and telephone services may find their market share declining.

Setting Up Outlook Express

You will use Outlook Express to create and send your e-mail message. To start Outlook Express,

- Choose Start/**P**rograms/Internet Explorer/Outlook Express.
- Enter your user ID and password to gain access to the Internet.
- Click [Read Mail].

> You can also click [icon] in the Quick Launch toolbar to start Outlook Express, or click [Mail] and choose Read Mail from within Internet Explorer.

The dialog box on your screen should be similar to Figure 3-1.

FIGURE 3-1

The Internet Connection Wizard is displayed. A **wizard** is a series of dialog boxes that guides you through the completion of a procedure. In this use, the wizard will help you set up or configure Outlook Express so that it knows the address of your Internet server, and your name and e-mail address. Without this information, Outlook Express does not know how to route or store your messages. To use the wizard to enter your preferences,

- Click **C**reate a New Internet Mail Account.
- Click **Next >**.
- In the Display Name text box, enter your real name. (This is the name that the recipient will see.)
- Click **Next >**.

> If your setup does not display the Internet Connection Wizard, your instructor will provide you with the instructions for setting preferences manually.
>
> The menu equivalent is **T**ools/**A**ccounts/**A**dd/**M**ail.

In the third wizard dialog box, you enter your e-mail address.

Concept 2: E-Mail Address

On the Internet, each person has a unique e-mail address or means of identification. The Internet uses an addressing system called the **Domain Name System (DNS),** which consists of three parts: a unique user name, a domain name, and a domain code, as shown below.

$$\underset{\text{user name}}{\text{oleary}} @ \underset{\text{domain name}}{\text{asu}} . \underset{\text{domain code}}{\text{edu}}$$

The user name identifies a particular user or group of users at a domain. It is separated from the domain name with the @ ("at") symbol. The domain name distinguishes a computer from a group of computers. The domain code identifies the type of use. The most common domains are commercial organizations or educational and research institutions. The domain code is generally a three-letter abbreviation; for example, edu stands for education and com for commercial. Periods, called dots, separate the domain name and code. The number of dots varies depending on how the address is structured for a particular computer.

> E-mail addresses are not case sensitive.

- Enter your complete e-mail address in the E-Mail Address text box.
- Click **Next >**.

The Wizard dialog box on your screen should be similar to Figure 3-2.

FIGURE 3-2

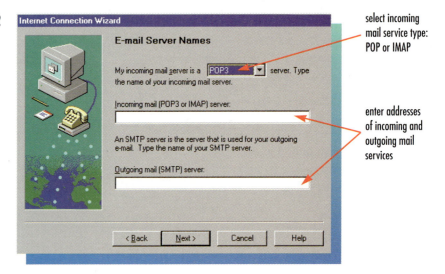

Next you need to specify the mail servers. These settings tell Outlook Express where to find the mail that has been sent to you.

Concept 3: Mail Server

Two mail servers work together to handle incoming and outgoing e-mail messages. The outgoing mail server uses the **Simple Mail Transport Protocol (SMTP)** to send messages over the Internet. The incoming mail server commonly uses either the **Internet Message Access Protocol (IMAP)** or the **Post Office Protocol (POP)** to deliver messages to your mailbox. Both have different advantages and disadvantages.

IMAP keeps messages individually in your mailbox on your incoming mail server. When you receive your mail, only the address and subject lines are downloaded to your computer. Then when you select a message to read, its content is downloaded. When you make changes to your messages, such as deleting messages, these changes are copied back from your computer to your mailbox on the incoming mail server. Therefore you always have access to an updated mailbox. The disadvantage to this system is if your connection to your server goes down while you are reading e-mail. Then only the current message is on your local computer and you must reestablish a connection before you can read more messages. Additionally, connect time is usually longer with IMAP because you must either be connected to the mail server while you are reading your messages, or you must reconnect every time you access a message you have not read.

POP copies entire e-mail messages to your computer all at once after you connect to the mail server. Therefore if you lose your connection, you still have all your messages. The major disadvantage is that when you make changes to messages stored in your computer mailbox, you must also make the same changes to the messages on your mail server's mailbox. If you do not synchronize both mailboxes, it can result in downloading new messages over and over (if you save your messages on your server) each time you connect, or can result in messages residing on computers you have previously used but to which you may not currently have access. The end result is you are sometimes unable to access all your messages when you need to.

- If necessary, select the appropriate mail server type as indicated by your instructor.
- Enter the incoming mail server and outgoing mail server information as provided by your instructor.
- Click Next >.

> If you are using a school computer, the mail server settings may already be entered correctly in the dialog box.

The wizard dialog box on your screen should be similar to Figure 3-3.

FIGURE 3-3

The next wizard step is to set the Internet Mail Logon for password-protected e-mail accounts. Your account name should already be entered based on the e-mail address you entered earlier.

- Enter your password for this account.
- Click Next >.

Outlook Express allows you to add a Friendly Name to your account.

- Enter your full name.
- Click Next >.

The remaining wizard screens ask you how you want to connect to the Internet.

- Follow the instructions provided by your instructor to complete these steps.
- Click Finish.

The wizard is closed, and the required settings to use Outlook Express are established. Next you will open your e-mail account.

- Click the Friendly Name of your e-mail account displayed in the list along the left edge of the window.
- If necessary, click Yes in response to the message dialog box to download IMAP folders for your new account.
- Click Inbox in the list on the left side of the window.

> Depending on how Outlook Express is configured at your school, each time you use a different computer to check your mail, you may need to enter your e-mail preferences.

Your screen should be similar to Figure 3-4.

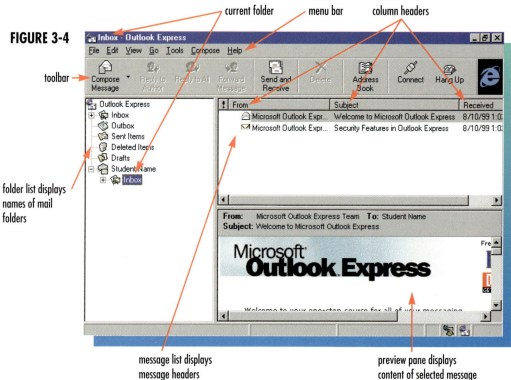

FIGURE 3-4

The Outlook Express window contains menus and toolbar buttons that are used to create and manage e-mail messages. These operate just as in Internet Explorer. The window is divided into three panes. The left pane, called the folder list, displays the list of folders where your e-mail messages are stored.

Concept 4: E-Mail Folders

Outlook Express includes several folders that are used to organize and store e-mail messages. The following table describes these folders.

Folder	Stores
Inbox	Incoming messages
Outbox	Messages that were not sent
Sent Items	Messages that were sent
Deleted Items	Messages that have been deleted
Drafts	Messages that you are still working on

In addition, if you are using an IMAP server, there are several folders created on that server to store your e-mail messages. Typically these will include an Inbox, a Saved-messages folder, and a Sent-mail folder.

You can also create your own folders on your hard disk to store different categories of messages. Organizing your messages can save you a lot of time when you are looking for a message sent or received some time ago.

The upper right pane displays the message list. It contains message header summaries that help identify each message. Typically the columns display the message priority, the name and/or e-mail address of the sender, the subject of the message, and the date and time the message was received. Additionally the message list may display the recipient's name, the size of the message, and the date the message was sent. The columns may also appear in a different order.

The lower right pane is the preview pane where the contents of the selected (highlighted) message are displayed. When you first use Outlook Express to access your mail account, you may receive an e-mail message welcoming you to Outlook Express similar to that shown in Figure 3-4. Otherwise, if you have not used your e-mail account before, your Inbox may be empty.

> Use **V**iew/**C**olumns to specify the columns to display and the order. You can also drag to change the column order.

> You may need to scroll the message list window horizontally to see the additional columns of information.

Composing an E-Mail Message

To create a new e-mail message,

- Click [Compose Message].
- Maximize the New Message window.

Your screen should be similar to Figure 3-5.

> The menu equivalent is **C**ompose/**N**ew Message, and the keyboard shortcut is Ctrl + N.

> The [Compose Message] drop-down menu displays options that can be used to select a stationery style on which to write your message.

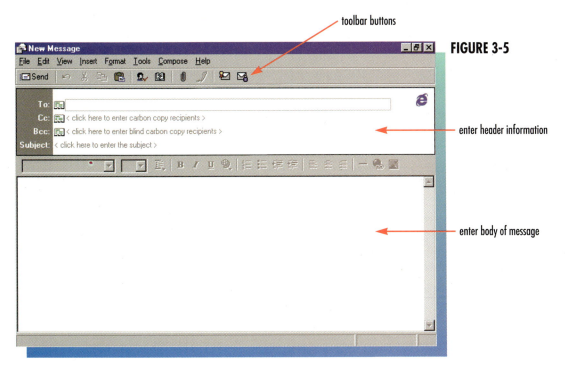

FIGURE 3-5

— toolbar buttons
— enter header information
— enter body of message

The New Message window is used to write, edit, and send e-mail messages. The toolbar buttons below the menu are shortcuts for menu options commonly used while creating a message. The upper section of the window contains the area where you enter the header information, and the lower section is where you enter the text for the body of your message.

Concept 5: Parts of an E-Mail Message

An e-mail message consists of two basic parts, the header and the body. The header consists of the lines at the top of the message that tell the computer where to send the message. It is similar to the format used in a standard memo. The body is the large blank area in the center of the screen where you type your message content. Most e-mail programs include basic word processing features to help you create and edit your message.

Typically the header consists of four lines: From, Date, To, and Subject. In addition, many headers include a line for attachments. These lines are described below.

- **From:** Contains the e-mail address of the sender of the message. This information is automatically entered for you.

- **Date:** Displays the date the message was sent.

- **To:** Contains the e-mail address of the recipient of the message. There are three different recipient types:

    To: Primary recipient of your message
    CC: Carbon Copy—for secondary recipients
    BCC: Blind Carbon Copy—for secondary recipients not identified to the other recipients, including those in the BCC list

- **Subject:** A brief description of the contents of the message. Although not required by Outlook Express, it is very helpful when you receive messages in reminding you of the content of the message.

- **Attachment:** An **attachment** is a text or non-text file, such as graphic file, spreadsheet, or Web page, that is sent along with your e-mail message. The attached file is downloaded to the recipient's computer where it can be opened using the specific software program.

In addition, one feature many people like to add to their e-mail messages is a **signature line** that is automatically added to the end of a message, much like a closing in a letter. Generally the signature line includes the sender's full name, postal address, phone number, fax number, and other e-mail addresses. Additionally the signature may include a quote or some other "signature" that is a means of showing a bit of your personality. You can add a signature line using **T**ools/**S**tationery/**S**ignature.

The first item you will specify in the header is the recipient. Every message must include this addressing information so the program knows where to send the message. You can enter an e-mail address, a nickname, a mailing-list name, or the name of a discussion group as the recipient. Most commonly, an e-mail address is entered. You want to send an e-mail message to your supervisor, Ramon Martinez, at The Sports Company.

- Type **rmartinez@www.mhhe.com**
- Click the Subject line to open the text box.

You are now ready to enter the subject for the message. The subject should be brief (many mailer programs will truncate long subject lines) and yet descriptive of the contents of the message. As much of the subject line as space allows will be displayed on the recipient's incoming message header. A subject line that pertains clearly to the e-mail body is a good way to get people in the right context to receive your message. To enter a subject for your message,

- Type **Suggestions for Web page**
- Click in the message area.

Your screen should be similar to Figure 3-6.

> You will learn about nicknames later in this lab, and about mailing lists and discussion groups in Lab 4.

> If the location of the recipient is on the same local area network as you, such as your school or business, you can shorten the e-mail address to the user name only.

> You can also press Tab to complete the entry and move to the next entry area. Do not, however, press ←Enter, as this creates another address line instead of moving to the next text box. To remove an extra address line, press Backspace.

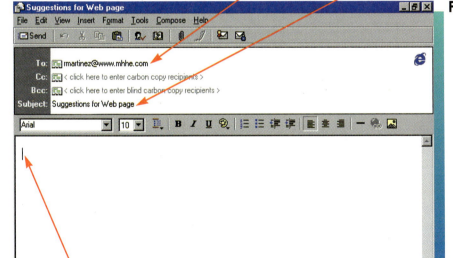

FIGURE 3-6

The insertion point appears at the left margin of the first line where you can begin to type your message.

Because of its speed and fast turnaround time, e-mail is fundamentally different from paper-based communication. In a paper document, it is absolutely essential to make everything completely clear and unambiguous because your audience may not have a chance to ask for clarification. With e-mail documents, your recipient can ask questions immediately. E-mail style thus tends, like conversational speech, to be much sloppier and more ambiguous. In addition, e-mail has its own guidelines for communication, called Netiquette.

Concept 6: E-Mail Style and Netiquette

E-mail is a fairly new way of communicating and has developed its own style and set of rules of courteous electronic communications called **Netiquette** (net etiquette). As a new user, you might be unaware of the meanings and subtleties of e-mail communication. The following are some e-mail style guidelines.

- When corresponding in a work or business situation, be careful what you write and how you write it. Spelling, grammar, and so on may not seem important at the time, but later you may regret any informality.

- In informal communications to friends and family, many people use special pictures of smiling or winking faces called **smileys** or **emoticons** to communicate feelings. They are created using combinations of characters, such as colons, hyphens, and parentheses.

Smiley	Meaning
:-)	Happy
:-(	Sad
;-)	Wink
:-P	Sticking tongue out
:-||	Angry
:-o	Shocked or amazed

Smileys are generally placed following the sentence in question. Other e-mail users enclose remarks in brackets such as <g> for "grin" and <jk> for "just kidding."

- In addition, in informal communications, many people use abbreviations for commonly used phrases to save typing time. Some examples are shown below.

Abbreviation	Meaning
ASAP	As soon as possible
FYI	For your information
PLS	Please
THX	Thanks

Abbreviation	Meaning
BTW	By the way
BCNU	Be seeing you
FWIW	For what it's worth
F2F	Face to face
IMHO	In my humble opinion
IRL	In real life
OBO	Or best offer
TNSTAAFL	There's no such thing as a free lunch
TTFN	Ta ta for now
TTYL	Talk to you later

It is easy to become too informal when using e-mail. It is still written communication, and like all written communication, the messages can be saved and printed. You can then be made accountable for your words.

The following are some Netiquette guidelines.

- Be concise. One of the many benefits of e-mail is its ability to answer a question or communicate a thought more quickly than a letter. Keeping e-mails short and to the point helps keep the recipient's attention and makes e-mail more productive.

- DO NOT TYPE YOUR MESSAGES IN ALL UPPERCASE CHARACTERS! This is called **shouting** and is perceived to be very offensive. Use a normal combination of uppercase and lowercase characters. Sometimes all lowercase is perceived as too informal or timid.

- If your e-mail program does not automatically word wrap, keep line length to 60 characters or less so your messages can be comfortably displayed on any type of monitor.

- Never send abusive, threatening, harassing, or bigoted messages. You could be held criminally liable for what you write.

- Think twice before sending your message: generally, once it is sent, you cannot get it back.

   Outlook Express contains a built-in text editor that helps you easily enter and edit your messages. Like a word processor, it includes a word wrap feature that automatically wraps the text to the beginning of the next line when the text reaches the right edge of the screen. Therefore you do not need to press ←Enter at the end of each line. Press ←Enter only when you need to end a line or to insert a blank line.

As in other Windows-based applications, the mouse, scroll bars, and directional arrow keys can be used to move through the message area.

Mouse	Action
Click new location	Positions insertion point
Click scroll arrow	Scrolls line by line or character by character in direction of scroll arrow
Click above/below scroll box	Scrolls document window by window
Drag scroll box	Moves multiple windows up/down

Key	Action
→	One character to right
←	One character to left
↑	One line up
↓	One line down
Ctrl + ←	One word to right
Ctrl + →	One word to left
Home	Beginning of line
End	End of line
Pg Up	Previous full window of text
Pg Dn	Next full window of text
Ctrl + Home	Beginning of message
Ctrl + End	End of message

To enter the message (type it exactly, including errors, as shown here),

- Type I have just *finnished* looking at the company's new Web page. It looks great and should be an excellent marketing tool when it is complete. You asked me to suggest how the newsletter page could be *imporved*. I would like to link the newsletter to another page, which will consist of links to Web sites containing information related to the articles in the newsletter. I took some time today to search for a few sites that could be included with this newsletter and have saved them to a file. I have attached the file Newsletter Links for you to look at.

> This message contains intentional typing errors. Do not be concerned if you make additional errors; you will learn how to correct them shortly.

Your screen should be similar to Figure 3-7.

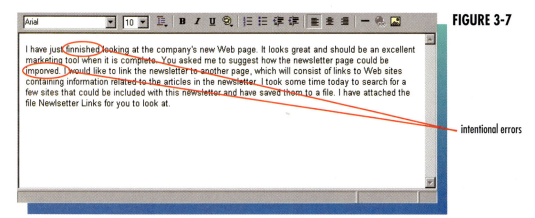

FIGURE 3-7

intentional errors

Checking Spelling

To ensure that your message does not contain spelling or typing errors, most e-mail programs include a spell-checking feature. To locate errors, the program checks each word in the message against a dictionary of words. If it cannot find a match, it highlights the word so you can edit it if needed. To spell-check this message,

- Choose **T**ools/**S**pelling.

Your screen should be similar to Figure 3-8.

The keyboard shortcut is F7.

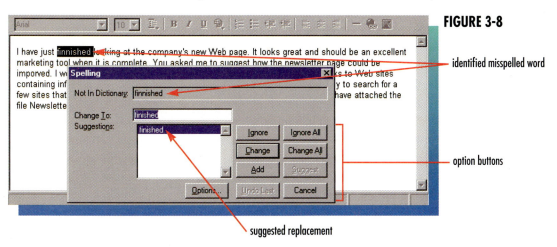

FIGURE 3-8

identified misspelled word

option buttons

suggested replacement

The Spelling dialog box is displayed, and the located misspelled word "finnished" is highlighted in the message. The Suggestions list box displays the words in the program's dictionary that most closely match the misspelled word. The first word is highlighted. Sometimes the Spelling feature does not display any suggested replacements because it cannot locate any words that are similar in spelling in the dictionary.

If the Spelling command is not available, this is because you do not have the necessary Microsoft Office program installed on your system. Skip this section and use the procedures covered in the "Editing a Message" section to correct these errors.

INTERNET EXPLORER 4

To tell the Spelling feature what to do, you need to choose from the following six options:

Option	Effect
Ignore	Accepts word as correct for this occurrence only.
Ignore All	Accepts word as correct throughout the spell-checking of the document.
Change	Changes word to the selected word in the Suggestions box.
Change All	Replaces word throughout the document with the word in the Suggestions box.
Add	Adds the entry in the Change To text box to the dictionary and replaces the selected word. If there are several entries in the Change To text box, each one is added to the dictionary.
Suggest	Displays the Suggestions list box.

> If there were no suggested replacements, and you did not want to use any of the option buttons, you could edit the word yourself by typing the correction in the Change To text box.

To change the spelling of the word to one of the suggested spellings, highlight the correct word in the list and then choose Change . Because "finished" is already highlighted and is the correct replacement,

■ Click Change .

Your screen should be similar to Figure 3-9.

FIGURE 3-9

corrected word

next located misspelled word

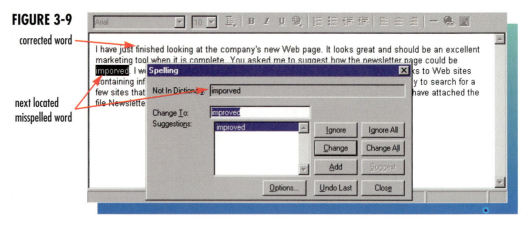

The Spelling feature replaces the misspelled word in the message with the correct spelling and continues to check the message for other errors.

■ Correct the spelling of any other words the program locates.

■ Click OK to end spell-checking.

Editing a Message

Before sending an e-mail message, you should reread it for accuracy and clarity. Having done this, you would like to edit your message by changing a few words. Some basic mouse and keyboard selecting and editing features are shown in the table below.

To select	Procedure
Word	Double-click in the word.
Multiple lines	Drag in the left margin next to the lines.
Paragraph	Double-click in the left margin next to the paragraph.
Multiple paragraphs	Drag in the left margin next to the paragraphs.
Entire message	Choose **E**dit/Select **A**ll

Editing Procedure	Button	Shortcut Key	Effect
		Backspace	Deletes character to left of insertion point or current selection.
		Delete	Deletes character to right of insertion point or current selection.
Edit/**U**ndo	↶	Ctrl + Z	Reverses last action or command.
Edit/**C**ut	✂	Ctrl + X	Removes selected text to Clipboard.
Edit/**C**opy	📋	Ctrl + C	Copies selected text to Clipboard.
Edit/**P**aste	📋	Ctrl + V	Pastes text from Clipboard.

> The Clipboard is a temporary storage area on your system.

- ■ Double-click the word "have" in the first sentence.
- ■ Press Delete.
- ■ Add the word "page" following the word "newsletter" in the fourth sentence.
- ■ Reread the message and use the editing features to correct any typing mistakes.

INTERNET EXPLORER 4

Formatting a Message

To enhance the appearance of your message, you can add formatting to your text. For example, you can change the font style and size, add color, bold, underlines, and italics. You can also emphasize important text with bullets and/or numbered lists, change the alignment of text, and insert objects such as pictures into the message. These features are mostly in the Format menu or on the Formatting toolbar located above the message area. Documents that include such formatting enhancements are called **rich-text documents.**

> The file extension .rtf identifies a file as a rich text formatted file.

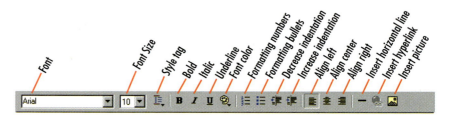

You would like to italicize the last sentence of the memo and bold the name of the file.

- Select the last sentence.
- Click Italic.
- Select the words "Newsletter Links."
- Click **B** Bold.
- Click in the last sentence to clear the highlight.

Your screen should be similar to Figure 3-10.

> Drag to select the sentence.

> The menu equivalent is F**o**rmat/**F**ont/St**y**le/**I**talic, and the keyboard shortcut is Ctrl + I.

> The menu equivalent is F**o**rmat/**F**ont/St**y**le/**B**old, and the keyboard shortcut is Ctrl + B.

FIGURE 3-10

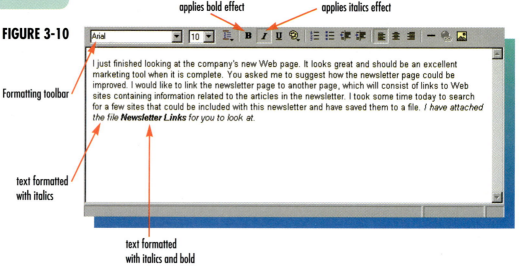

The sentence is now displayed in italics and the file name is bold. You can add as many enhancements as you like to a message. But keep in mind that, as with any other type of document, too many enhancements can clutter a document and make it hard to read.

Attaching Files

The last thing you need to do before sending this message is to attach the file to the message. The ability to send files attached to your e-mail message is a very convenient feature. For example, if you are working on a group project you can e-mail your section of the project to another member of your group. This makes it easy to get information to each other without having to meet in person. You can attach files of any type, including text, sound, graphics, and Web pages. For the attachment to be read by recipients, they must have the appropriate software program.

- Click Insert File.

The Insert Attachment dialog box on your screen should be similar to Figure 3-11.

> Refer to Concept 5 for a description of an attachment.

> You can send a Web page that you are viewing in an e-mail message using **F**ile/**S**end/**P**age By E-mail in Internet Explorer. The New Message window is opened with the page already embedded. Just address and send.

> The menu equivalent is **I**nsert/File **A**ttachment.

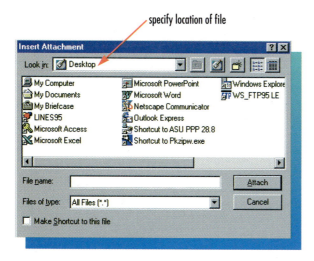

FIGURE 3-11

From this dialog box you identify the file you want to attach. This is similar to the File Open dialog box you have used in other applications to open a document. The text file you want to attach is the file you created in Lab 2 and saved on your data disk.

- From the Look In drop-down list, select the drive that contains your data disk.
- Select Newsletter Links.rtf.
- Click  .

> If the Newsletter Links file is not available, use Related Links.rtf on your data disk.

Your screen should be similar to Figure 3-12.

FIGURE 3-12

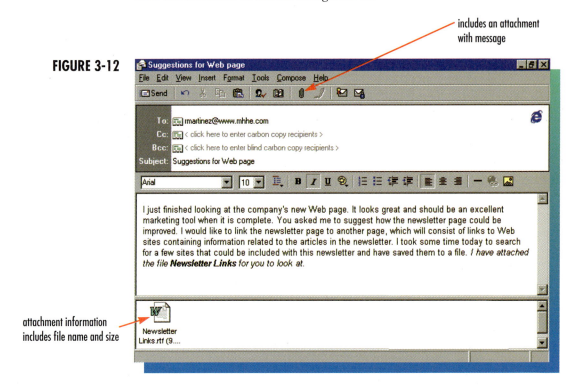

includes an attachment with message

attachment information includes file name and size

> **Point to the attachment to see this information displayed in a screen tip.**

Notice that the file name you just selected, along with its size, is displayed in the Attachment section of the message. When you send this message, a copy of the file will be sent along with the message.

Sending a Message

Now that your message is complete, you can send it.

- Click Send.

> **If a Send Mail message dialog box appears, indicating your message will be placed in the Outbox for later delivery, click OK, then click Send and Receive.**

How do you know the message was sent? Always assume that it was. If it is not sent, it is bounced back to you with a message from your mail administrator indicating the reason why. The most common reason is an incorrectly entered e-mail address.

> **The menu equivalent is File/Send message.**

Opening an Attachment

The New Message window is closed, and the Message List window is displayed again. When Outlook Express sends a message, it automatically keeps a copy of the message for you in the Sent Items folder on the hard disk.

> **If your messages are long and you are paying for online time, you may find it useful to create the messages offline. Use File/Send Later to save the message in the Outbox folder to be sent when you get online.**

- Click the Sent Items folder in the folder list.
- If necessary, click on the message header of the message you sent.

Your screen should be similar to Figure 3-13.

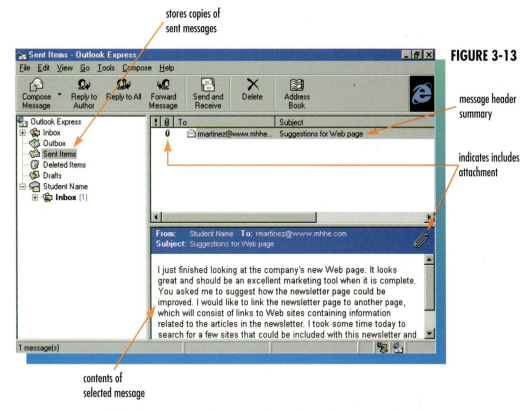

FIGURE 3-13

The Sent Items folder has the same layout as the Inbox. The message list displays the message header summary, and the contents of the selected message are displayed in the preview pane. The message appears exactly as it will appear when received by the regional manager. The 🔗 to the left of the message header and the 📎 in the upper right corner of the preview pane indicate the message includes an attachment.

- Click .

A button with the file name of the attachment is displayed. To open an attachment, you click on the button. If your system recognizes the file format (identified by the file extension), it will open the appropriate application and display the file. If it does not recognize the file type, you must save the file and then open it using the correct software program.

WARNING!

Open only attachments whose source you trust. Protect your computer by using a virus-checker program to check the attachment before opening it on your computer. Then, if you are unsure of an attachment, save it to your disk rather than open it so that the virus-checker program can check it first.

■ Click [Newsletter Links.rtf (7.52 KB)].

Your screen should be similar to Figure 3-14.

FIGURE 3-14

If necessary maximize the word processor window.

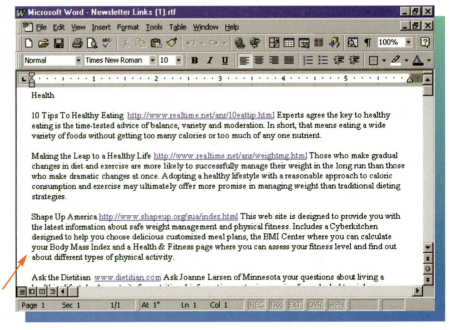

attachment opened in word processor

Because your system recognizes this file as a rich-text file from the file extension .rtf, the word processor on your system is automatically loaded and the file of Web sites is displayed.

■ Click [X] in the title bar to close the file and exit the word processor program.

Checking Incoming Mail

After checking your message, you decide to see if you have received any new mail. When you load Outlook Express, it automatically checks for incoming mail. Also, by default the program checks for new mail every 30 minutes. You can check for mail manually by clicking [Send and Receive] at any time.

Your system may play a sound to announce the arrival of a new message.

Checking Incoming Mail **IE97**

- Open your personal Inbox folder.
- Click [Send and Receive].

The menu equivalent is **T**ools/**S**end and Receive, and the keyboard shortcut is Ctrl + M.

A message box is briefly displayed that advises you of the number of new messages waiting to be delivered and the progress of the delivery as the messages are downloaded to your computer.

If no new messages are displayed, wait a few minutes and try again.

While you were checking out the Sent Items folder, a reply message from the regional manager was received and should be displayed in the message list. The status bar shows a count of the total number of messages in the folder and the number that have not been read.

- If necessary, click on the reply message header from the regional manager.

Your screen should be similar to Figure 3-15.

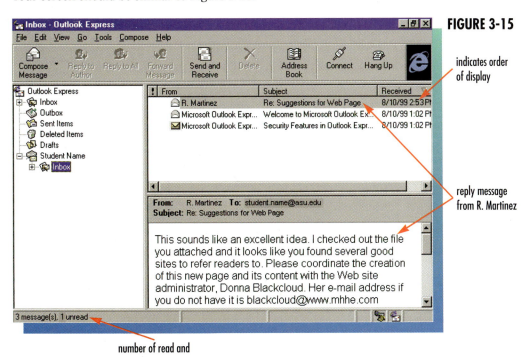

FIGURE 3-15

indicates order of display

reply message from R. Martinez

number of read and unread messages

When the Inbox contains a lot of messages, it is often convenient to arrange the messages in an order that makes it easy for you to locate a specific message. They can be sorted by any column category. Most commonly, messages are sorted by date received in ascending or descending date order. The triangle symbol in the column heading points up △ to indicate ascending order and down ▽ to indicate descending order. You want to display the most recently received messages at the top of the list.

To help you locate messages, you can also use the **E**dit/**F**ind Message command. It allows you to enter a keyword to search on and to specify which parts of messages you want to search.

You may need to scroll the message list pane to see the Received column.

- If necessary, click the Received column header (to change the date order to descending ▽).

The menu equivalent is **V**iew/Sort **B**y/Received/**A**scending.

The reply message from the regional manager should be displayed at the top of the message list. The information in the Inbox message header is essentially the same as in the Sent Items folder except that the sender's rather than the recipient's name or e-mail address is displayed, and the Received column shows the date the message was received. You read messages in the Inbox folder just as you do in the Sent Items folder.

Notice that the mail icon to the left of the message header is an open letter 📖, which indicates that the message has been read. This icon appears as a closed letter ✉ when the message has not been read.

Many times when there are many new messages, you may want to see more message headers so you can selectively read them. To do this you can turn off the display of the folder list and preview pane.

> When a message header is highlighted, the mail icon automatically changes to 📖 after a preset number of seconds (5 is the default). Use **E**dit/Mark as U**n**read to change the message status back to unread.

- Choose **V**iew/**L**ayout.

- Click Fol**d**er List

- Click Use **p**review pane.

The Window Layout Properties dialog box on your screen should be similar to Figure 3-16.

FIGURE 3-16

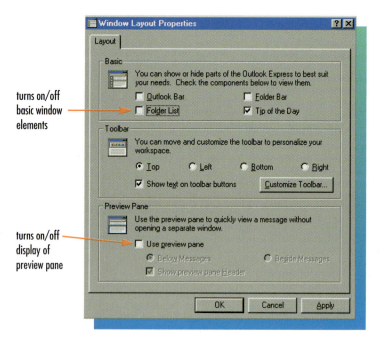

- Click OK .

Your screen should be similar to Figure 3-17.

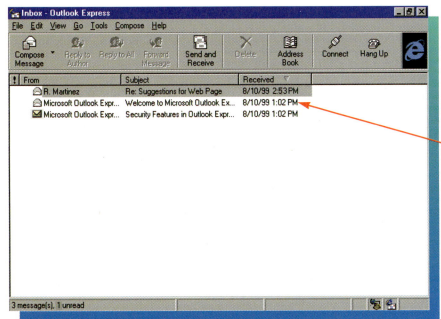

FIGURE 3-17

folder list and preview pane are closed to allow message list to occupy entire window space

The preview pane and folder lists are closed. To display messages in this view, you would double-click on the message header to display the message in a separate window. To display the preview pane again,

- Choose View/Layout/Use preview pane.
- Click OK.

You can also adjust the size of the message pane to display more or less of the message header window by dragging the divider between panes downward. If you drag too far down, only the message header is displayed.

If the message is long, you can use the scroll bar to read it or you can double-click on the message header to display the message in a separate message window. Then you do not have to scroll as often to read the message.

- Double-click the message header for the message from the regional manager.
- Maximize the window.

Your screen should be similar to Figure 3-18.

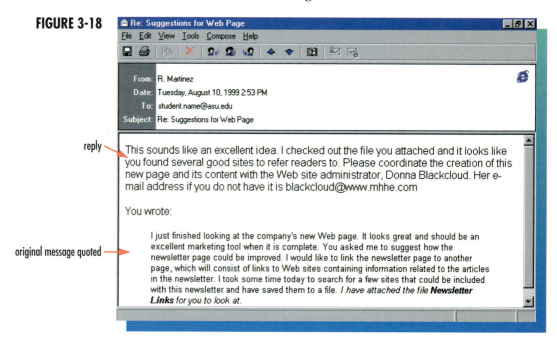

FIGURE 3-18

Notice that the regional manager has included the full contents of your message in his reply to you. This is called **quoting** and provides the recipient with a frame of reference as to what the message reply is about. The new text of the message appears above the quote.

Creating an Address Book

The regional manager's reply includes the e-mail address of the Web administrator for The Sports Company site. You need to contact this person about the new page and make plans on how to proceed. Since you will probably be working closely with this person, you decide to add the e-mail address to your address book.

Concept 7: Address Book

Rather than trying to remember many different e-mail addresses, you can create a file of addresses called an **address book.** Then when you select a name from the address book, the e-mail address is automatically entered in the To header line. Using the address book is like speed-dialing a phone number, and like speed-dialing, it is faster and more accurate.

Entries in the address book include the person's full name, a nickname, their e-mail address, organization, and title. A **nickname** is an easy-to-remember shortcut for a person's e-mail address. It can be entered in the To header line and Outlook Express will replace it with the e-mail address when the message is sent. This is helpful when you send a lot of mail to the same person. You can also specify with each address whether they can receive plain-text-only formatted messages. When this information is included in the address book, the message is automatically sent to that person in the specified format.

In addition, you can create a mailing list consisting of a list of names in the address book. The list is assigned a name that is added to the address book as an alias. Then by entering the mailing list name in the To header line, you can quickly send the same message to all the people on the list.

Usually you add an address to the address book by typing it in directly or by copying it from the message header of a message you received. In this case, because the address is included in the message you are viewing, you will copy it from the message to the address book.

- Select Donna Blackcloud's e-mail address and click 📋 to copy it to the Clipboard.
- Click 📖 Address Book.
- Click [New Contact].

> The menu equivalent is **T**ools/**A**ddress **B**ook, and the keyboard shortcut is Ctrl + Shift + B.

The Properties dialog box on your screen should be similar to Figure 3-19.

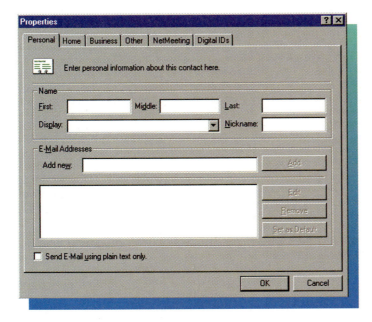

FIGURE 3-19

In the Personal tab of this dialog box you enter the individual's personal information.

- Click in the Add ne**w** text box and press Ctrl + V (the Paste shortcut) to enter the e-mail address.
- Complete the remaining text boxes using the information shown below:

    First name: **Donna**

    Last name: **Blackcloud**

    Nickname: **Donna**

- In the Business tab, enter the information shown below:

  Company: **Southwest Regional office**

  Job title: **Web Administrator**

- Click [OK].

The Address Book window on your screen should be similar to Figure 3-20.

FIGURE 3-20

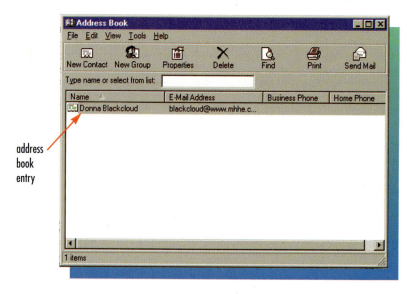

> To delete an address book entry, select the address and click [Delete].

The new address entry is added to the address book. Next you will add the regional manager's address to the book. Another way to add an address is to copy the header information from a message you have received.

- Switch to the mail message window.
- Right-click on the name in the From line and select A**d**d To Address Book from the shortcut menu.

A new address form is displayed with the sender's e-mail address automatically completed for you.

- Complete the Personal tab by entering the nickname **Manager.**
- Complete the Business tab by entering the information shown below:

  Company: **Southwest Regional office**

  Job title: **Regional Manager**

- Click [OK].

> Addresses appear in alphabetical order in the address book by default.

> Pointing to an address entry displays information about the addressee in a screen tip.

- Finally, add your instructor's e-mail address and information to the address book.
- Close the Address Book window.

Replying to E-Mail

When you are finished reading a message, you can either reply to it, forward it, file it, delete it, or just leave it. Many times you will want to reply to the message. When the message header is highlighted or you are viewing the message, it is not necessary to type in the recipient's address and subject information. The Reply command will automatically enter the sender's address as the recipient for you. You will reply to the message from Mr. Martinez (you should be viewing it).

- Click Reply to Author.
- If necessary, maximize the window.

Your screen should be similar to Figure 3-21.

> The menu equivalent is **C**ompose/**R**eply to Author, and the keyboard shortcut is Ctrl + R.

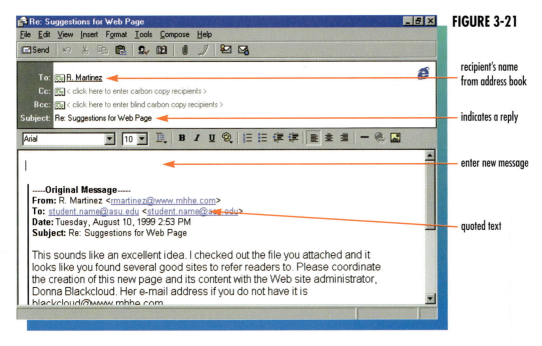

FIGURE 3-21

- recipient's name from address book
- indicates a reply
- enter new message
- quoted text

The name of the recipient as it is recorded in the address book is automatically displayed in the To text line. It is a link to their e-mail address contained in the address book.

If the recipient was not in the address book, the e-mail address from the recipient's original message would appear in the To text line. The original subject text is entered following Re: in the Subject line. Outlook Express automatically quotes the entire original message by copying it into the body of the reply. The quoted text is preceded with a line in the left margin. If the original message is long and you are replying to only part of the message, edit the quoted text to include just enough to provide a context for the message and no more. Then add your own new message to the reply, just as you did when composing a new message.

An insertion point appears above the quoted text. If the contents of the quoted message are important to the answer, put your new text below the quoted text; otherwise place any new text above the original message. You will add your reply to the beginning of message.

- Type **I will contact Donna Blackcloud today. The new Web page should be ready by the end of next week.**
- Press [←Enter] twice.
- Proofread and spell-check the message.
- Click [Send].

After the message is sent, you are returned to the Inbox.

Forwarding a Message

Next you want to send Donna a copy of the original message you sent to the regional manager. Another convenient feature of e-mail is the ability to **forward** a message to another person. All that is needed when forwarding a message is to specify the address of the new recipient. The e-mail program automatically includes the text of the message you are forwarding, saving you from having to retype the same information. You will use the address you entered in your address book to forward the message to Donna.

- To open the Sent Items folder, choose **G**o/**G**o To Folder/Sent Items/[OK].
- Select the message header line of the original message you sent to the regional manager.
- Click [Forward Message].
- Maximize the window.

> The keyboard shortcut is [Ctrl] + Y.

> The name of the current folder is displayed in the title bar.

> The menu equivalent is **C**ompose/**F**orward and the keyboard shortcut is [Ctrl] + F.

Your screen should be similar to Figure 3-22.

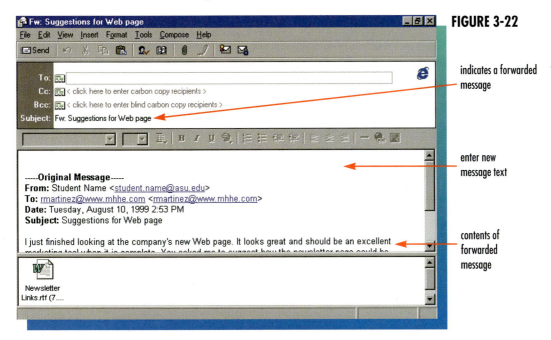

FIGURE 3-22

The subject line displays "Fw:" along with the original subject. The contents of the original message and the attachment are displayed in the message area. The To line is blank so you can enter the address of the person you want to forward the message to. You will use Donna's nickname to enter her e-mail address from the address book in the To text line.

- Type **D** in the To text box.

Notice that Outlook Express automatically completes the name for you, much as it completes URLs. You will also send a copy of this message to your instructor. To enter that e-mail address,

- Click 📖 Select Recipients.

> If there are multiple nicknames in the Address Book beginning with the same letter, you will need to type additional letters until the correct address is located.

The Select Recipients dialog box on your screen should be similar to Figure 3-23.

FIGURE 3-23

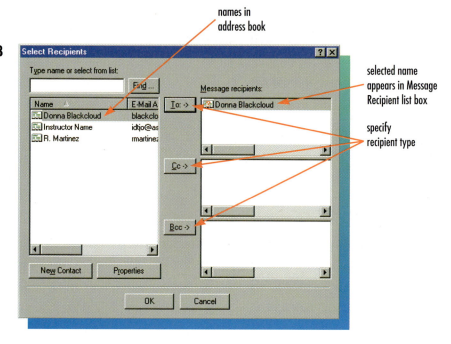

The menu equivalent is **T**ools/Select **R**ecipients.

Remove a selected recipient by selecting the name and pressing Delete.

- Select your instructor's e-mail address.
- Click Cc -> .
- Click OK .

The name of your instructor appears in the Cc line. This is much faster than typing the entire address, and also minimizes errors when typing complicated e-mail addresses.

You can add text to the existing message, just as you would if composing a new message or replying to a message. You will add a brief message of your own in the body above the forwarded message text.

- Click above the original message in the message area.
- Type **I am forwarding a copy of a message I sent to Mr. Martinez about my suggestion for a new Web page on the company Web site. He has asked me to coordinate the creation of this page with you. Are you available any time tomorrow morning to discuss how to proceed?**
- Press ←Enter twice.
- Type your name.
- Press ←Enter.
- Proofread and spell-check the message.
- Send the message.

The message is forwarded to the recipient.

Saving a Message

Some messages you receive will contain information that you will want to keep or take with you to another location. You can save these messages in a folder you create or as a file on a disk. This is called **archiving.** You will save the reply message from the regional manager to your data disk.

- Redisplay the Folder List (**V**iew/**L**ayout/Fol**d**er List).
- Open your Inbox.
- Select the message header of the reply you received from the regional manager.
- Choose **F**ile/Save **A**s.

In this box you specify the location to save the file, the file name, and the file type. The default file type of Mail is correct. Using this format you can open the file using any mail program.

- If necessary, select the drive that contains your data disk.
- Enter **Reply** as the file name.
- Click .

The file is saved on your data disk.

Deleting a Message

Other messages, once read, are no longer needed. To clear your Inbox of unneeded mail, you can quickly delete messages. You will delete the message you just saved.

- If necessary, select the message header of the reply you received from the regional manager.
- Click [Delete].

If your Inbox messages are stored on an IMAP server, the deleted message icon appears as [icon], indicating it is marked for deletion. Alternatively, the deleted message may appear to have been immediately removed from the Inbox. If this is the case, you can turn on the option to display messages marked for deletion.

> The menu equivalent is **E**dit/**D**elete, and the keyboard shortcut is [Ctrl] + D.

> Use **E**dit/**U**ndelete to restore an item marked for deletion.

Corresponding Using E-Mail

- You can also use drag and drop to move messages to different folders to help organize your messages.

- The Inbox must be selected for this option to be available.

- You can also use Tools/Options to set Outlook Express to automatically remove deleted files on exiting the program.

■ If necessary, choose View/Current View/Deleted Messages.

If your Inbox messages are stored on your hard disk, they are immediately removed from the Inbox and transferred to the Deleted Items folder. This is similar to Windows Recycle Bin. You can view messages in the Deleted Items folder just like any other folder. If you want to restore a message that is in the Deleted Items folder to the Inbox, you can drag the message header to the appropriate folder in the folder list. To permanently remove the message,

■ Choose Edit/Purge Deleted messages.

When you permanently remove messages, Outlook Express automatically compacts the other folders to a size just large enough to hold the remaining mail.

Printing a Message

Finally, you will find there are many times that you will want to print a copy of a message. You will print the message you sent to Donna Blackcloud.

■ If necessary, prepare your printer to print.

■ Open the Sent Items folder.

■ Select the message header of the message to Donna Blackcloud.

■ Choose File/Print.

- The keyboard shortcut is Ctrl + P.

■ If necessary, select the appropriate printer for your system.

■ Click OK.

■ When you have completed this lab, click ✖ to exit Outlook Express.

■ If necessary, disconnect from the Internet.

- The menu equivalent is File/Exit.

LAB REVIEW

Key Terms

address book   (IE100)
archive   (IE107)
attachment   (IE84)
Domain Name System (DNS)   (IE79)
e-mail   (IE77)
emoticon   (IE86)
forward   (IE104)
Internet Message Access Protocol (IMAP)   (IE80)

mailbox   (IE77)
mailer program   (IE77)
mail server   (IE77)
Netiquette   (IE86)
nickname   (IE100)
Post Office Protocol (POP)   (IE80)
quote   (IE100)
reader program   (IE77)
rich-text document   (IE92)

shout   (IE87)
signature line   (IE84)
Simple Mail Transport Protocol (SMTP)   (IE80)
smiley   (IE86)
store-and-forward   (IE77)
wizard   (IE79)

Command Summary

Command	Shortcut Key	Button	Action
File/**P**rint	Ctrl + P		Prints selected message
File/E**x**it			Exits Outlook Express
Edit/**D**elete	Ctrl + D		Deletes selected item
Edit/**U**ndelete			Restores deleted item
Edit/Pu**r**ge Deleted Messages			Permanently removes deleted messages
Edit/Mark as U**n**read			Changes message status to unread
Edit/**F**ind Message	Ctrl + Shift + F		Finds messages in current folder
View/Current **V**iew/D**e**leted Messages			Displays messages that have been marked for deletion
View/**C**olumns			Specifies columns to display and location
View/Sort **B**y			Changes column to sort on and order of sort
View/**L**ayout			Changes display of window elements
Go/**G**o to Folder	Ctrl + Y		Selects a folder to go to
Tools/**S**end and Receive	Ctrl + M	Send and Receive	Gets e-mail messages from server and sends any outgoing e-mail
Tools/**A**ddress Book	Ctrl + Shift + B		Opens address book
Tools/**A**ccounts/**A**dd/**M**ail			Configures Outlook Express mail
Tools/S**t**ationery/**S**ignature			Creates a signature line
Tools/**O**ptions			Specifies configuration settings
Compose/**N**ew Message	Ctrl + N	Compose Message	Creates a new e-mail message
Compose/**R**eply to Author	Ctrl + R	Reply to Author	Returns e-mail message to sender's address
Compose/**F**orward	Ctrl + F	Forward Message	Sends e-mail message to new address
New Message Window			
File/**Se**nd Message		Send	Sends message immediately
File/Send **L**ater			Stores message in Outbox to be sent later
Edit/**U**ndo	Ctrl + Z		Reverses last action or command
Edit/Cu**t**	Ctrl + X		Cuts selected text to Clipboard

Command	Shortcut Key	Button	Action
Edit/**C**opy	Ctrl + C	📋	Copies selected text to Clipboard
Edit/**P**aste	Ctrl + V	📋	Pastes text from Clipboard
Edit/Select **A**ll	Ctrl + A		Selects entire document
Insert/File **A**ttachment		📎	Attaches file to e-mail message
Format/**F**ont/**S**tyle/Italic	Ctrl + I	*I*	Italicizes selected text
Format/**F**ont/**S**tyle/Bold	Ctrl + B	**B**	Bolds selected text
Tools/**S**pelling	F7		Starts spell-checking feature
Tools/Select **R**ecipients		📖	Selects recipients from address book

Matching

1. Match the following with their definition or function.

1) shouting   _____ a. electronic mail communications over a network

2) archive   _____ b. a happy emoticon

3) e-mail   _____ c. a text or non-text file that is attached to an e-mail message

4) header   _____ d. to send a message on to another recipient

5) doleary@mckenna.com   _____ e. rules of courteous e-mail communication

6) forward   _____ f. to save a message

7) :=)   _____ g. message entered in all uppercase letters

8) attachment   _____ h. addressing information of an e-mail message

9) Netiquette   _____ i. text of an e-mail message

10) body   _____ j. an e-mail address

Fill-In Questions

1. In the following Outlook Express screen, identify the parts by entering the correct term for each item.

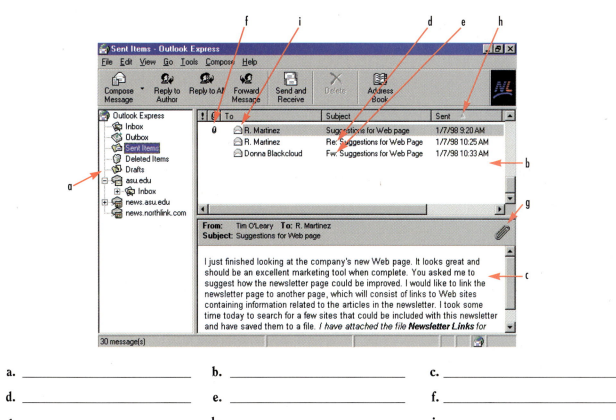

a. _____ b. _____ c. _____
d. _____ e. _____ f. _____
g. _____ h. _____ i. _____

Discussion Questions

1. What is e-mail? How is e-mail used?
2. What is store-and-forward technology?
3. What is the standard format of an e-mail address?
4. What is an attachment? How do you know if your message includes an attachment? How do you view an attachment?
5. What is a signature line?
6. What are the rules of courteous e-mail correspondence called? Discuss three rules and why they are important.
7. How can you express feelings when corresponding using e-mail? Give three examples.
8. Discuss several sources you can use to find an e-mail address.
9. Discuss the advantages of creating an e-mail address book or recipient list.
10. What are some problems associated with e-mail?

IE112 Corresponding Using E-Mail

Hands-On Practice Exercises

Step by Step

1. Damon Lembi works for a computer training company. He has access to the Internet and needs information on when a new product is going to be available. He would like to send an e-mail message to his contact at a software supply company.

a. Start Outlook Express and compose the following new message:

   To: <your user name@domain name>
   Subject: Release of new product

   Jack,

   I am interested in finding out when you expect to receive the next upgrade of the word processing program I am currently using. I would like to begin preparing class materials so we are ready to go as soon as the product is available. Any help you may be able to provide is appreciated.

   Thanks, <your name>

b. Carbon copy your instructor.
c. Spell-check the message and edit as needed.
d. Send the message.
e. Print a copy of the message.

2. Joanne Clark uses e-mail to keep in contact with her outside sales representatives. She needs to send a message to two representatives that are attending a conference in another city.

Note: Your instructor will provide you with the e-mail address to complete this problem.

a. Compose the following message:

   To: <user name@domain name>,
   CC: <your user name@domain name>
   Subject: New reporting procedure

   Hope you are enjoying the conference.

   I need to let you know that the company is implementing a new procedure for reporting sales orders. A new form has been designed to help us keep track of the increase in reorders by specific customers.

   The new forms will be delivered to your hotel by FedEx this afternoon. If you have any questions about the new forms, send me a message and I will get back in touch with you.

   Have fun and don't get too much sun.

   Joanne Clark

b. Spell-check the message and edit as needed.
c. Send the message.

   Wait for the message to be placed in your mailbox. You would now like to reply to Joanne's message and ask her about the new forms.

d. Enter the following reply.

   Joanne,

   Do you want the orders that have not been submitted yet transferred to the new forms?

   <your name>

e. Send the message. Print the message.

3. You would like to practice adding names to your address book.

a. Collect e-mail addresses from several friends, family, or classmates.
b. Add their names, e-mail addresses, and nicknames on new cards.
c. Select one of the names from the address book and compose a new message.

d. Before sending the message, you would like to carbon copy (CC) the message to your instructor. Use the address book to enter your instructor's address in the CC line.

e. Send the message. Print the message.

4. While working on The Sports Company Web page, you found many links to fitness- and health-related issues. You would like to inform the manager about your ideas for the next newsletter, which is being designed for the next quarter focusing on health and fitness issues for children.

a. Start Internet Explorer and search for information on health and fitness issues for children. Create a document in a word processor that contains the Web addresses and short descriptions of pages that would be appropriate for the newsletter.

b. Compose a new e-mail message addressed to rmartinez@www.mhhe.com. Use the subject Next Quarter Newsletter Ideas. Include a CC to your instructor's e-mail address.

c. Enter a body of the message informing Mr. Martinez about the information and letting him know you are attaching a file with more information.

d. Attach the word processor file of Web page descriptions you created.

e. Send your message. Print the message.

On Your Own

5. Practice composing and sending messages by sending a message to a classmate. Have a classmate send a message to you. When you receive the message from your classmate, reply to it. Print your reply. Forward the message to another classmate.

6. In Lab 2 you learned how to search for e-mail addresses. If you have not already done so, complete Practice Exercise 3 in Lab 2. Use Four11 to locate your address or a friend's address. To create an address card directly from Four11, select the name and from the personal Web page choose Get vCard. Click the [New Contact] button to open the address card. Complete any additional information. Close the address card and send a message to the address. Next, use the Edit/Find People command in Outlook Express to locate another person and create an address card for this person. (Use Help for information about this feature.)

Concept Summary

Corresponding Using E-Mail

How E-Mail Works
E-mail requires the use of two programs: a mailer program and a delivery system.

Mail Server
Two types of mail servers work together to handle incoming and outgoing e-mail messages.

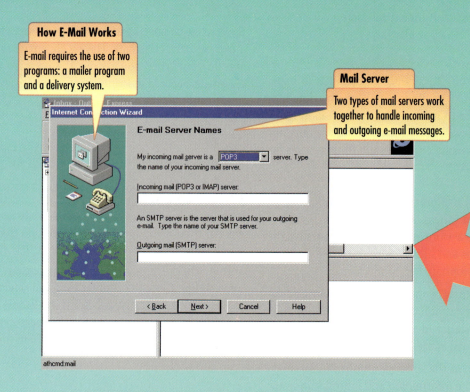

E-Mail Address
On the Internet, each person has a unique e-mail address or means of identification.

Parts of an E-Mail Message
An e-mail message consists of two basic parts, the header and the body.

E-Mail Style and Netiquette
E-mail is a fairly new way of communicating and has developed its own style and set of rules of courteous electronic communications called Netiquette (net etiquette).

E-Mail Folders

Outlook Express includes several folders that are used to organize and store e-mail messages.

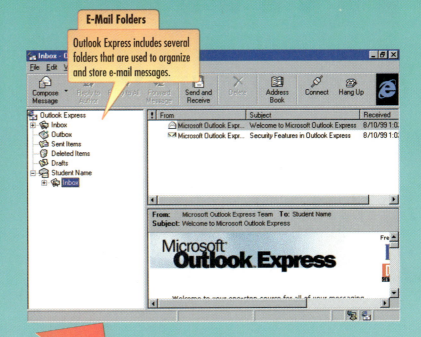

Concepts

- How E-Mail Works
- Mail Server

- E-Mail Folders

- Parts of an E-Mail Message
- E-Mail Address
- E-Mail Style and Netiquette

- Address Book

Address Book

Rather than trying to remember many different e-mail addresses, you can create a file of addresses called an address book.

115

4 Communicating with Newsgroups, Mailing Lists, and Chat Groups

COMPETENCIES

After completing this lab, you will know how to:

1. Find and subscribe to newsgroups.
2. Read a newsgroup message.
3. Post a message to a newsgroup.
4. Reply to a newsgroup message.
5. Unsubscribe to newsgroups.
6. Search for newsgroup topics.
7. Find and subscribe to mailing lists.
8. Join a chat discussion.

CASE STUDY

The Internet consists of many parts in addition to the World Wide Web. One large part that has been in existence much longer than the Web is the ability to communicate with others using e-mail. Another form of communication is through discussion groups that allow you to participate in interactive, ongoing discussions about a topic of common interest with people from all over the world.

During your search for Web sites that contain information related to the newsletter content, you came across references and links to discussion groups. You think that it may also be useful to include links in the related topics links page to several discussion groups whose topic is related to information in the newsletter. You decide to use Microsoft Internet Explorer to locate and learn how to communicate in the different types of discussion groups.

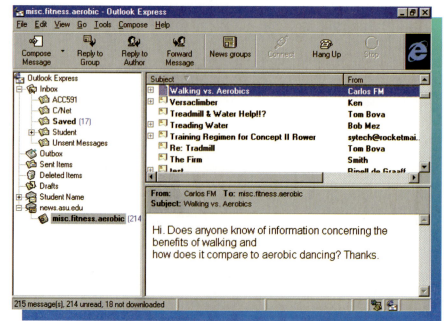

Finding and Subscribing to Newsgroups **IE117**

Concept Overview

The following concepts will be introduced in this lab:

1. **Newsgroup** — Newsgroups are special interest groups that are part of the network news system called Usenet, a network dedicated exclusively to the dissemination of newsgroup messages.

2. **Categories of Newsgroups** — Usenet organizes newsgroups into categories called hierarchies.

3. **Thread** — A thread is a newsgroup discussion about a specific topic with a common theme.

4. **Newsgroup Culture** — Newsgroups tend to develop personalities over time. The members get to know one another and think of their group as not just a location, but a place where they can talk with friends.

5. **Mailing List** — Mailing lists consist of the e-mail addresses of a group of people who have subscribed to the mailing list because they are interested in the topic of the group.

6. **Subscription Address and List Address** — The subscription address is used to perform administrative tasks with the listserver, and the list address is used to communicate with mailing list members.

7. **Chat Group** — Communicating in a chat group means carrying on a conversation live (in real time) with other people over the Internet.

Finding and Subscribing to Newsgroups

Discussion groups allow you to communicate with groups of people who have similar interests. They provide a great way to exchange ideas and information. They may not always offer accurate information, but they are generally a rich resource for learning about a topic. Three very popular types of discussion groups are newsgroups, mailing lists, and chat groups. Newsgroups and mailing lists rely on e-mail to exchange information, while chat groups allow direct "live" communication.

INTERNET EXPLORER 4

First you decide to look for newsgroups that may be discussing topics related to the articles in the newsletter.

> ### Concept 1: Newsgroup
>
> **Newsgroups,** also simply called groups, are special interest groups that are part of the network news system called **Usenet,** a network dedicated exclusively to the dissemination of newsgroup messages. Usenet distributes most, although not all, messages via the Internet. Newsgroup participants correspond using e-mail, but unlike e-mail, messages are not sent to your personal inbox but to newsgroup sites for anyone to read. A **newsgroup site,** also called the **news server,** is a computer that participates in the Usenet network. Each site receives one copy of messages, called **articles,** which are sent or **posted** by the newsgroup members. The articles are stored on the site's disk, and after a period of time are removed. The length of time articles are stored is controlled by the news administrator at the site. The news administrator also decides what newsgroups to carry.
>
> There are two types of newsgroups, moderated and unmoderated. In **moderated** newsgroups articles are sent to the moderator, who reviews or screens them for appropriateness before they are distributed. In **unmoderated** newsgroups the articles are not screened. Anyone can start an unmoderated newsgroup on any topic. Generally they consist of open and uncensored discussions.

> Usenet is short for User's Network and is often spelled in all capital letters.

> A large number of newsgroups are not part of Usenet. Their distribution is not as wide and they may not be carried by all Internet service providers.

> It is estimated that there are more than 20,000 Usenet newsgroups, with new ones being added all the time (and others being removed).

To access newsgroups, you use a **newsreader program.** This program allows you to read newsgroup messages and presents them in an organized fashion. The newsreader program is included in Outlook Express.

- Start Outlook Express.

- Click 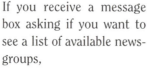 from the Outlook Express folder.

> The menu equivalent is <u>G</u>o/<u>N</u>ews.

- If necessary, complete the Internet Connection Wizard as you did in Lab 3 to configure the Outlook Express newsreader. You will be asked for the NNTP server address at your school. Your instructor will provide the necessary information.

> The NNTP server is the computer that handles newsgroup messages.

If you receive a message box asking if you want to see a list of available newsgroups,

> You can also click 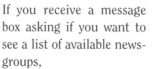 and choose Read News to open the newsreader program from within Internet Explorer.

- Click  .

Your screen should be similar to Figure 4-1.

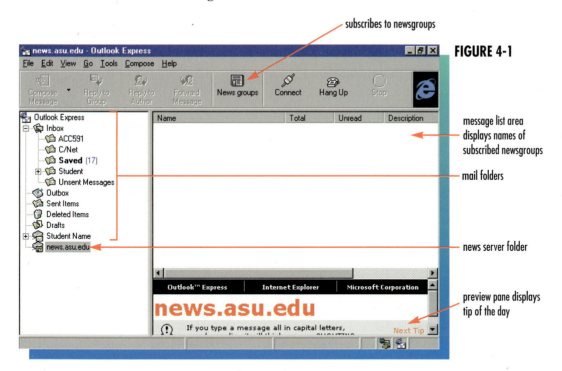

FIGURE 4-1

Outlook Express displays your mail and news folders in the folder list. When you first use Outlook Express to read newsgroups, the news folder is empty. Your first step is to join or **subscribe** to the newsgroups you would be interested in reading. Although you do not need to subscribe to a newsgroup to read the messages, you must subscribe if you want to participate in the discussion. Subscribing only means that you are marking the newsgroup, much as you would add a Web page to your Favorites list, to make it easier to access.

■ Click  .

The list of available newsgroups is downloaded to your system if this is the first time Outlook Express has been used to access newsgroups.

> Your News folder displays the name of the news server at your school.

> Your News folder may display newsgroup names in the message list pane if previous users subscribed to newsgroups.

> The menu equivalent is **T**ools/News**g**roups.

The Newsgroups dialog box on your screen should be similar to Figure 4-2.

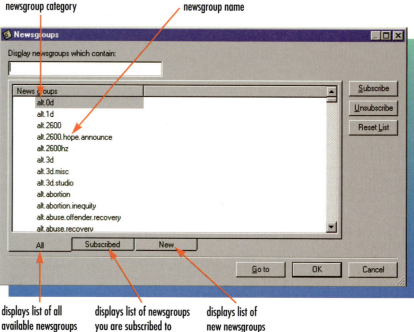

FIGURE 4-2

- newsgroup category
- newsgroup name
- displays list of all available newsgroups
- displays list of newsgroups you are subscribed to
- displays list of new newsgroups

The three tabs in this dialog box can be used to list all available newsgroups (All), subscribed newsgroups (Subscribed), and newsgroups created since you last listed available groups (New). The All tab is open by default and displays the names of all newsgroups on the news server. To help locate newsgroups, Usenet has organized them into categories.

Concept 2: Categories of Newsgroups

Usenet organizes newsgroups into categories called **hierarchies.** There are about 30 major top-level hierarchies. The top-level hierarchy is then further subdivided into additional categories. The top seven hierarchies are often referred to as the "Big Seven." They are described below.

Hierarchy	Description
comp	Computers
misc	Discussions that do not fit anywhere else
news	Discussions about Usenet itself
rec	Recreation
soc	Social issues
sci	Science
talk	Controversial topics

In addition, one of the most popular top-level hierarchies beyond the Big Seven is alt (for alternative), which includes miscellaneous discussions that generally inspire a lot of different opinions.

Each newsgroup has a multipart name that reflects the hierarchical organization. The names (from left to right as you read them) display the top-level hierarchy first, separated from the next (subtopic) by a dot, and so on. Therefore as you read the newsgroup name, the various parts of the name progressively narrow the topic of discussion. A sample of some newsgroups and what they discuss is shown below.

Newsgroup Name	Topic
alt.romance	Romance-related discussions, such as how to ask someone out
alt.tv.3rd-rock	"Third Rock from the Sun" television program
rec.food.recipes	Recipe exchange
rec.travel	Basic travel advice and tips
comp.unix.questions	Questions on the Unix operating system
comp.windows	Discussions on the Windows operating system
comp.edu	Computer science education
soc.politics	Political problems, systems, solutions
soc.feminism	Feminism and feminist issues
news.announce.important	Important messages to all Usenet users
news.answers	FAQs (frequently asked questions) on Usenet
news.announce.newusers	Standard set of articles with general information about Usenet

Because the news administrator decides which newsgroups to carry, not all of these newsgroups may appear on your news server.

You want to locate a newsgroup that discusses fitness topics. A good category in which to look for this group is the misc.category. Although you could find newsgroups in this category by scrolling the complete list of newsgroups, it is much faster to narrow the list to topics you are interested in first.

■ Type **misc.** in the Display Newsgroups Which Contain text box.

> You can also find a specific newsgroup by typing the entire newsgroup name in the Display Newsgroups Which Contain text box.

INTERNET EXPLORER 4

Your screen should be similar to Figure 4-3.

FIGURE 4-3

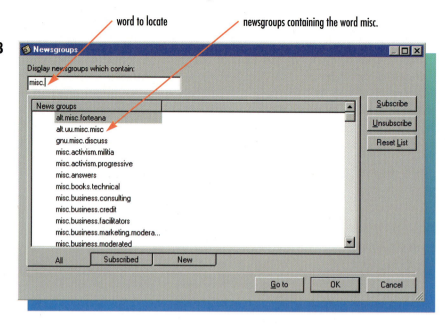

Now the list displays only those newsgroups containing the word "misc." You will further narrow the list to display newsgroups also containing the word "fitness."

- Type **fitness** in the text box.
- If necessary, select the misc.fitness.aerobics newsgroup.
- Click **Subscribe**.

> You can also double-click the newsgroup name to subscribe.

The newsgroup name is marked with a 🗞 icon, indicating you have subscribed to it. The dialog box remains open so you could continue to subscribe to other groups if you wished. To complete the process for this group only,

- Click **OK**.

> Clicking **Go to** immediately opens the selected newsgroup and downloads messages without subscribing to the group.

Your screen should be similar to Figure 4-4.

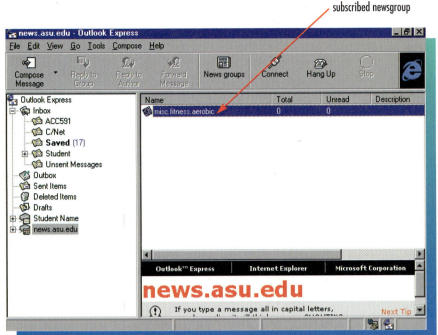

FIGURE 4-4

Reading Newsgroup Messages

The Outlook Express newsgroup window now displays the name of the subscribed newsgroup in the message list pane. The main reason for subscribing to newsgroups is to read and reply to messages from other group members. To download the messages in this newsgroup,

- Double-click misc.fitness.aerobic.

After a few moments the messages are downloaded, and the message count is displayed in the status bar. The name of the subscribed newsgroup also appears in the folder list. The window displays the messages in a similar manner to the e-mail window. The message headers are displayed in the message list pane, and the contents of the selected message are displayed in the preview pane.

- Click on any message header to display the message content.

> If a message box appears advising you that there are new newsgroups, click Yes to download them and then click Cancel to close the dialog box.

> If there are a lot of messages in the newsgroup, it will take a long time to download them.

> By default, the first 300 messages are downloaded.

Your screen should be similar to Figure 4-5.

FIGURE 4-5

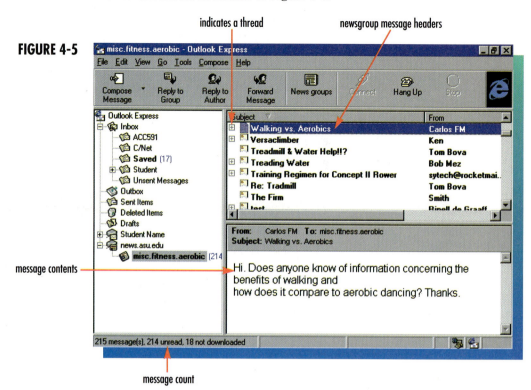

The message header includes the topic for each message in the Subject column, the name of the person who submitted the message in the From column, the date the message was posted in the Sent column, and the size of the message in the Size column.

Message headers preceded with a ⊞ indicate that there are responses to the original message. This creates a thread of topics in the newsgroup.

> Different message headers will be displayed on your screen.

> You can change the size of the panes and move and size columns just as in Outlook Express Mail.

Concept 3: Thread

A **thread** is a newsgroup discussion about a specific topic with a common theme. Threads help organize subtopics in a newsgroup and are used to keep all the messages on the same subject together. When an original message is posted, it begins a new thread. All responses or follow-up messages are attached to the original so that you can read all the messages on the same subject one after the other.

■ Click on the ⊞ preceding any message to display the message thread.

You will probably see several message subject headers that begin with "Re:". This indicates that the message is a response to an original message, thereby creating a discussion thread.

■ Click on an original message to read it and follow the thread through the replies.

Your screen should be similar to Figure 4-6.

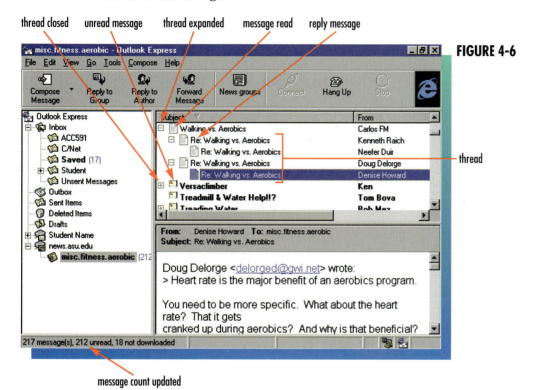

FIGURE 4-6

As you select each message, the contents are downloaded from the server and displayed in the preview pane. Also notice after you have selected a message, the preceding the message header changes to . This indicates the message has been read. Additionally, the count of total and unread messages in the status bar is updated. You can also manually mark a message as read or unread, mark a thread as read, mark all messages as read, and mark messages from a specific date as read or unread using the Edit menu.

Posting a Message to a Newsgroup

As you read messages in a newsgroup, you may come across a question for which you have an answer or a topic on which you have an opinion. You may also have a new topic you want to discuss. Before posting to a newsgroup, you should be aware of the culture of the group.

> Double-click on the message header to display the message in a separate, full-size window.

Concept 4: Newsgroup Culture

Newsgroups tend to develop personalities over time. The members get to know one another and think of their group as a place where they can talk with friends. And much like any friendships, there are cliques with traditions. Before jumping in with questions or answers, it is a good idea to get a feel for the newsgroup first by reading messages for a few days. This is called **lurking.**

In addition, you may want to check out the newsgroup's **FAQ** (Frequently Asked Questions) article. This article contains answers to the group's most frequently asked questions. Reading the FAQ before posting a question saves the group from having to answer the same question repeatedly. FAQs also often include an explanation of abbreviations that you will frequently see used in the group. Some of the commonly used abbreviations and their meanings are listed below.

Abbreviation	Meaning
SO	Significant other
AFAIK	As far as I know
IMHO	In my humble opinion
OIC	Oh, I see!
TIA	Thanks in advance

As with e-mail, you will also find newsgroup messages that contain inflammatory remarks, called **flames.** This often leads to a thread called a **flame war.** When presented with a post that is meant to enrage you, the best thing is to ignore it and delete it. Another negative dynamic you will find in newsgroups is called **trolling.** This is the deliberate posting of a message containing incorrect information with the intent of receiving know-it-all replies.

Some other newsgroup terms are described in the table below.

Term	Meaning
Spam	The annoying practice of sending junk e-mail (such as an advertisement) to newsgroups or mailing lists or to anyone you do not know.
RFD	Before a new group is created, Request for Discussion topics are proposed and voted on and will be widely propagated.
Saint	Someone who provides helpful information to new users and informs others of proper procedures within a group.
Wizard	Someone who has a great deal of knowledge about how things work.

Before posting a message to any newsgroup, you may want to practice the procedure first. For this purpose, many news servers offer a test newsgroup. You will practice posting a message in a test newsgroup.

- Click [News groups].

- Type **test** in the text box.

- Subscribe to the misc.test newsgroup.

- Click misc.test in the folder list to download the newsgroup messages.

To post a new message to this newsgroup,

- Click [Compose Message].

- Maximize the window.

Your screen should be similar to Figure 4-7.

> All newsgroups containing the word "test" are listed.

> Your instructor will give you the name of the newsgroup if it is different from the one used in this text.

> The menu equivalent is **C**ompose/**N**ew Message, and the keyboard shortcut is Ctrl + N.

> The [Compose Message] drop-down menu can be used to select a stationery style on which to write your message.

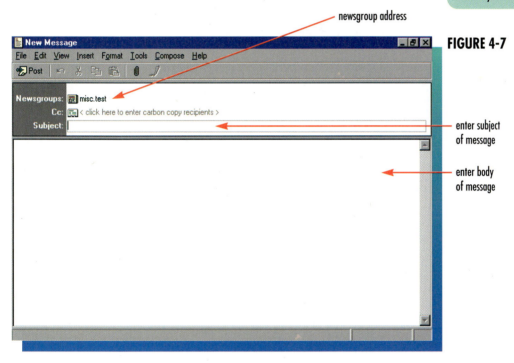

FIGURE 4-7

The New Message window is open. Creating a posting is similar to creating an e-mail message. It consists of header, subject, and message areas. And as with e-mail, there are some rules of etiquette that you should follow when posting a message.

Newsgroup Etiquette

In general, the same rules of etiquette apply. However, because you are posting to a public group, several other considerations should be kept in mind.

- When posting replies, keep them brief and to the point, being particularly careful to stick to the topic thread.

- Before you reply to a message, read the rest of the messages in the newsgroup to confirm that no one has already said what you want to say. If someone has, do not repeat it.

- One of the biggest problems on Usenet is that a single question often receives many identical answers, unnecessarily overburdening the system. E-mail your answer directly to the person who asked the question and suggest that they summarize their responses to the group.

- Likewise, when you post a question, suggest that answers be sent to your e-mail address and offer to summarize the answers to the group so others can benefit as well. The best way to summarize is to strip headers, combine duplicate information, and write a short summary. Try to credit the information to the people who sent it to you, where possible.

- When replying to a message, summarize the parts to which you are responding by including appropriate quotes from the original message. Then readers do not have to try to remember what the original message said.

Notice that the name of the newsgroup has already been entered for you in the Newsgroups line, just as when replying to an e-mail message. You can post a message to multiple groups by adding additional newsgroup addresses. This is just like sending the same e-mail message to multiple people.

The Subject line is important to complete, because this line's content is what is displayed in the subject area of the message header. Because the subject line of a message is there to help a person decide whether or not to read your message, it is important that it be descriptive of the contents of the message. In addition, it should be brief and to the point.

- In the Subject line type **Test Message Ignore.**

By entering "ignore" in the subject line, you will not get an automatic e-mail reply from the newsgroup's news server. If you leave it out, you may receive an e-mail message telling you that your test message was received.

The text of your posting is entered in the message area, just as if you were typing an e-mail message. You can also add formatting to the text and include an attachment with the message. Because most test messages are not read by anyone other than the original sender, if you ask a question you more than likely will not get an answer.

- In the message area type **This is my test message.**
- Click **Post**.
- If necessary, click **OK** in response to the Post News message box.

> If a message appears indicating the message will be placed in the Outbox to be sent later, use **F**ile/**S**end Message or Alt + S to send it immediately.

The message is sent to the news server and posted to the newsgroup to which it is directed. It may take seconds to hours or days before the message is displayed in the newsgroup. Just like other newsgroups, test messages are removed from the server periodically and can only be deleted by the server administrator or the person who posted the message. Because Usenet posts are intended for a public audience, never post anything you would not feel comfortable reading in the newspaper.

> To cancel a message you have posted, select the message in the newsgroup and choose **C**ompose/**C**ancel Message. Until the server deletes the message, others can still read it.

To see the message you posted to the newsgroup,

- Choose **T**ools/Download **th**is Newsgroup.

The Download Newsgroup dialog box is displayed. To download new message headers only,

- Select **G**et the Following Items.
- If necessary, select New **H**eaders.
- Click **OK**.

Any new messages sent to the newsgroup since you last opened it are added to the message header list. Since there are usually a large number of messages in a newsgroup, it could take a long time to locate one message or find the one that relates to topics that interest you. Because of this you can sort the messages by subject, sender, date, or size. Since you just recently sent your message, sorting by descending date order should put your message at the top of the list.

> You may need to scroll the message list pane horizontally to see the Sent column.

> The triangle symbol in the Sent header will be ▽ when the order is descending.

> The menu equivalent is **V**iew/Sort **B**y/Sent/Ascending (clears the option).

- If necessary, change the sort order of the Sent column to descending.
- Select your message header.

> If your message header is not displayed, repeat the process to download new messages again. If it still is not posted, select any other test message.

Your screen should be similar to Figure 4-8.

FIGURE 4-8

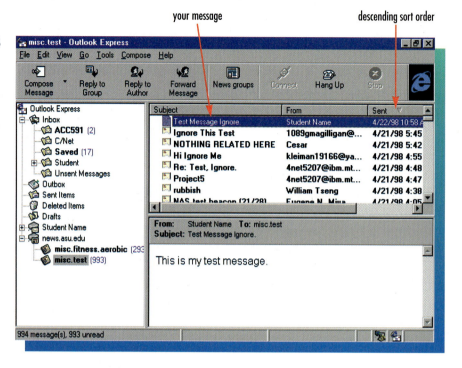

Replying to a Newsgroup Message

As with e-mail, you can also reply to a newsgroup message. You can reply directly to the sender's e-mail address, to the sender and all other recipients' e-mail addresses, to the newsgroup, or to the sender and newsgroup. You will create a reply to the newsgroup.

> The menu equivalent is **C**ompose/Reply to Newsgro**u**p, and the keyboard shortcut is Ctrl + G.

- Click

Notice that the address and subject lines have been completed for you, and the insertion point is waiting for you to enter additional information. The original message text is also quoted. To complete your reply,

- Type **Testing my reply.**
- Click **Post**.
- If necessary, click **OK**.
- Load the new messages into the newsgroup.

Your reply should be displayed in the newsgroup as a thread below your original message.

- Read and then print your reply message.

Unsubscribing to Newsgroups

Since you no longer need the newsgroups, you will unsubscribe to them.

- Click [News groups].
- Open the Subscribed tab.
- Select the misc.test newsgroup.
- Click [Unsubscribe].
- Click [OK].

A faster way to unsubscribe is to choose the command from the newsgroup's shortcut menu.

- Right-click on the misc.fitness.aerobics newsgroup in the folder list to display the shortcut menu.
- Choose Unsubscribe from this newsgroup.
- If necessary, click [Yes].
- If you are asked if you want to view a list of newsgroups, click [No].

You can always resubscribe to a newsgroup at any time if you later decide you want to check what is going on in the group.

After watching the information flow in various newsgroups for awhile, you will feel comfortable posting your messages and questions. This may lead to gathering names and exchanging information with many people in different areas of the world. You can also print, copy, cut, and paste messages using the menu commands just as in other Windows applications.

- Close Outlook Express.

> The menu equivalent is **T**ools/Unsub-sc**r**ibe from this newsgroup.

Searching for Newsgroup Topics

As you have seen, Usenet is a huge conglomeration of newsgroups with far-ranging topics of discussion. It is sometimes difficult to know which category to look in to locate a newsgroup you may be interested in. In addition, because postings are cleared periodically from the news server, you may miss a topic that was discussed that is of interest to you. To help find newsgroups and articles on specific topics, you can use a specialized Web search site such as Deja News or a search service such as AltaVista, which allows you to select just Usenet as the area to search. To find other newsgroups that may be discussing aerobics, you will use AltaVista.

- Start Internet Explorer.
- Enter **altavista.digital.com** in the Address box.
- Click the Search Usenet link in the far right corner of the Search box.

> You can also access a newsgroup by typing its URL in the Address box. URLs for newsgroups begin with "news" rather then "http," followed by the newsgroup name. There is no server name or path.

> You can also display AltaVista in the Search Explorer Bar.

- Type **aerobics** in the search text box.
- Click Search.
- Scroll the window to see the search results.

Your screen should be similar to Figure 4-9.

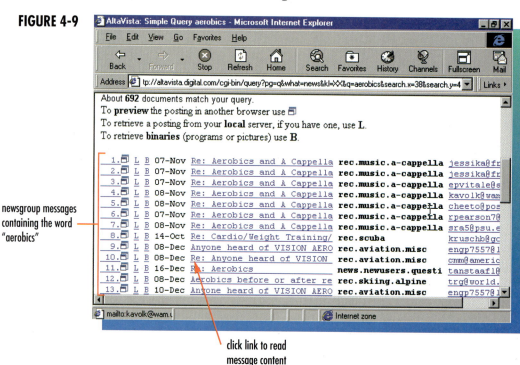

FIGURE 4-9

newsgroup messages containing the word "aerobics"

click link to read message content

A list of messages matching your search query is displayed. The most relevant messages are at the top of the list. As you can see, the topic of aerobics was discussed in many other newsgroups in addition to the misc.fitness.aerobic newsgroup.

- Click on the subject link of any message to read it.
- Click Back to return to the AltaVista search results page.

In addition to reading postings, you can also reply directly to the sender by e-mail by clicking on their e-mail address link. This opens the Outlook Express New Message window where you can create and send your message. You cannot, however, at this time reply to the newsgroup through AltaVista.

> You can click the newsgroup name when viewing the message to subscribe and view current articles.

Finding Mailing Lists

Next you want to check out another popular type of discussion group, mailing lists, for discussions on fitness-related topics.

Concept 5: Mailing List

Mailing lists, also referred to simply as lists, consist of the e-mail addresses of a group of people who have subscribed to the mailing list because they are interested in the topic of the group. The messages are sent to a single e-mail address, where they are then forwarded to each subscriber's e-mail inbox to read. There are roughly 40,000 mailing lists on specialized topics from environment to presidential politics to cooking. Each list has a set of subscribers, with varying levels of expertise and interest in the list topic. As with newsgroups, there are both moderated and unmoderated mailing lists.

Although most mailing lists are on the Internet, many are on the **Bitnet,** an academic network founded in 1981 to link universities by e-mail. The Internet and Bitnet networks are connected by a specialized computer called a **gateway,** which translates e-mail messages sent from one network into the protocol used on the other network. Because Bitnet relies heavily on e-mail to move information, you must communicate via e-mail to the mailing lists.

Most mailing lists are managed by automated computer programs, the most common of which is a **listserver,** called **listserv** for short. The listserv is responsible for the mechanics of accepting subscriptions to the list and of forwarding messages to subscribers on the list. It also allows subscribers to temporarily put a hold on deliveries and to unsubscribe from the list.

> Other mailing list computer programs are majordomo and listproc.

To subscribe to a list, you must locate the name of the list and the subscription address. One source of mailing list topics is through commercial publications, such as the Internet Yellow Pages published by McGraw-Hill. Several online sources are also available that provide mailing list topics. One such source is available by sending an e-mail message to listserv@listserv.net, a master list of mailing lists organized by topic. Leave the subject line of the message blank. At the top of the message body, enter "list global <topic>", where <topic> is a word or words describing the subject. For example, to get a list of mailing lists on space, you would enter "list global space." You will receive by e-mail a list of all known listservs relating to space.

You can also use the Web search engines to conduct a search for mailing lists on specific topics. There are also many Web pages devoted to maintaining a list of mailing lists on specific topics. The following Web sites help you locate e-mail lists. Some offer keyword searching, some provide information about the list, and some let you subscribe right from their Web site.

Communicating with Newsgroups, Mailing Lists, and Chat Groups

Web Site	Description
L-Soft Listserv Lists http://www.lsoft.com/lists/listref.html	Enables you to search for discussion lists by topic, name, or host sites. Includes a listing of lists with over 1,000 subscribers (not complete).
Interest Groups Finder http://alabanza.com/kabacoff/Inter-Links/listserv.html	Provides links to resources for finding e-mail discussion groups.
Tile.Net http://www.tile.net/tile/listserv/index.html	You can browse lists alphabetically by host country, see which ones are most popular, and conduct subject searches.
Liszt http://www.liszt.com/	A searchable directory of mailing lists with over 23,000 entries.
Publicly Accessible Mailing Lists http://www.neosoft.com/cgi-bin/paml_search/	An up-to-date index of mailing lists arranged alphabetically by name and by subject.

You will use the L-Soft Listserv Lists Web site to locate a mailing list about exercise. To access this page,

- Enter **www.lsoft.com/lists/listref.html** in the Address box.
- Click the link **Search** for a mailing list of interest.
- Type **exercise** in the Look For text box.
- Click **Start the search!**.
- Click on the link to the search result, FIT-L@MAELSTROM.STJOHNS.EDU
- Scroll the page to see the information on how to subscribe.

> If this URL does not work, try http://www.lsoft.com/catalist.html.

> If this mailing list is not listed, select another of your choice.

Your screen should be similar to Figure 4-10.

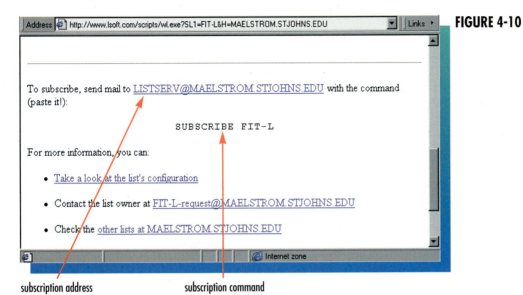

FIGURE 4-10

This page includes information about the mailing list, its size, and how to subscribe. This looks like a site that may be of interest to readers. Before recommending it, however, you want to subscribe to it so you can see what topics are being discussed.

Subscribing to Mailing Lists

To participate in a mailing list, you first must become a member by subscribing to the list. You subscribe to a mailing list by sending an e-mail message to the subscription address.

> **Concept 6: Subscription Address and List Address**
>
> The **subscription address,** also commonly called a **listserv address,** of a mailing list is used to perform administrative tasks such as subscribing, unsubscribing, and requesting information from the listserv program. The subscription address consists of <listserv>@ followed by the listserv address.
> The **list address** of a mailing list is used to send a message to the members of the mailing list. The list address consists of <list name>@ followed by the last part of the subscription address.
> (continued)

Concept 6 (concluded)

It is important to understand the difference between the listserv address and the mailing list address. You send commands to the listserv address and posts to the mailing list address. Perhaps the most common problem on mailing lists is that people unintentionally send listserv commands to the mailing list address rather than to the listserv address. This fills up the mailing list with the electronic equivalent of junk mail that no one wants to see.

Those groups that are on the Bitnet use a Bitnet address. Bitnet addresses are different from Internet addresses in that they do not end in geographical or administrative domain names, such as .edu. Generally, all that is needed to send an e-mail message from the Internet to the Bitnet is to add .bitnet to the end of the address. Otherwise you may need to provide the name of the gateway computer and information about how to deliver the mail on Bitnet. Some Bitnet listservs are also connected to the Internet, so if you see a listserv address ending in .edu, you can e-mail the listserv without adding .bitnet to the end.

The Web page shows the subscription address for the list is listserv@maelstrom.stjohns.edu with the command "subscribe FIT-L." The command is entered in the body of your e-mail message and tells the listserver which mailing list you want to join. To subscribe, you can click the link in the Web page.

 Click LISTSERV@MAELSTROM.STJOHNS.EDU.

Your screen should be similar to Figure 4-11.

> If you selected a different mailing list, substitute the appropriate commands in the following steps to subscribe.

FIGURE 4-11

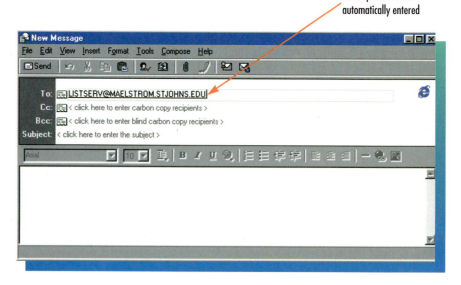

subscription address automatically entered

The Outlook Express New Message window is open, and the subscription address is automatically entered in the To line for you. In your e-mail subscription message, you enter the command to subscribe. When corresponding with the listserv, because you are communicating with a computer program, only certain commands are acknowledged. Because listserv programs vary, different commands may be used by different listservs. Many of the commands that can be used when sending an e-mail message to most listservs are listed below.

Listserv Command	Action
subscribe <listname>	Subscribes to list.
unsubscribe <listname>	Unsubscribes to list.
signoff <listname>	Unsubscribes to list.
review <listname>	Requests a membership list.
index <listname>	Requests names of files that are archived on the list.
info <listname>	Requests information about the listserv.
get <filename>	Requests a copy of an archived file.
set <listname> nomail or postpone	Temporarily stops mail delivery.
set <listname> mail or mailback	Begins mail delivery again after stopping.
set <listname> repro	Has listserv send a copy of whatever you post to list.

The most common command to begin a subscription is "subscribe." The command is followed by the name of the mailing list. The name for the mailing list is Fit-L. In some cases the mailing list name is then followed by your name. Do not use your e-mail address, because the listserv gets it from your message header. To enter the command and send the message,

- Type **subscribe fit-l** in the message text area.

Your screen should be similar to Figure 4-12.

> You can move the New Message window to see the instructions in the browser window on how to subscribe.

> You can copy and paste the subscription message into the New Message window.

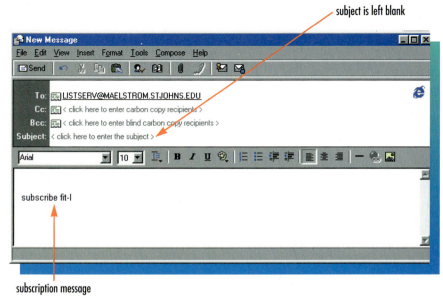

FIGURE 4-12

The subscription message is complete.

- Click  to send the message.

You are asked if you want to include a subject. When subscribing to mailing lists, the subject line is ignored, so leave it blank.

- Click .

Generally, in a matter of a few minutes, you will receive any number of different e-mail responses back from the listserv. One message may tell what computer resources were used to process your subscription. There may be an interim message telling you that your subscription request has been received and that it will be processed shortly or that it is being forwarded. If your subscription request contained an error, you will receive a message indicating what is wrong. In that case you would need to resubmit your request. Some mailing lists send a message asking you to send a confirmation response to the listserv. If you receive this type of message, you would need to follow the instructions to confirm your subscription.

- While waiting for your reply, open your inbox and get your incoming mail messages.

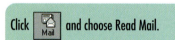 Click and choose Read Mail.

Note: If you do not receive a reply in 10 minutes, continue reading the information in this section. Before ending the lab, check your inbox for replies to your subscription request and perform the instructions in this section.

If your subscription request to the mailing list went through without any problems, you will receive a reply rather quickly. This message will be a confirmation message.

- Read the command confirmation request message.

Your screen should be similar to Figure 4-13.

FIGURE 4-13

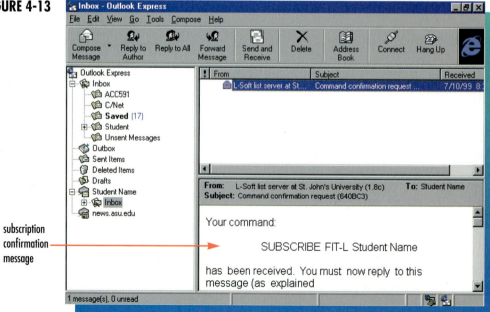

subscription confirmation message

Because we do not want to clutter the mailing list with unnecessary subscriptions, you will not send in the confirmation. Your request will then be canceled automatically when no response is received within 24 hours.

If you had confirmed the request, you would receive two more replies. The first message would indicate that you have been added to the mailing list. The second message would welcome you to the list and provide additional information about the list, including information on how to unsubscribe. You always want to save a copy of this message so you will know how to unsubscribe to the list at a later time.

> If the mailing list you subscribed to did not require confirmation, follow the steps to unsubscribe.

- **Print a copy of your confirmation message, and then delete all mailing list messages.**
- **Close Outlook Express.**

Once you have subscribed, your e-mail address is added to the list of subscribers to the mailing list and you will receive copies of all e-mail messages sent to the mailing list. Depending on how active the list is, you may begin receiving messages immediately and you may find that your inbox is flooded with e-mail messages from the mailing list. When you first subscribe, you may want to observe and find out what the list is about before participating. Each list has its own personality.

After waiting a few days and reading some of the messages from the mailing list, if you find you are interested in a topic, post a message to the mailing list (use the list address). In this case you would address your e-mail message to fit-l@maelstrom.stjohns.edu. Remember, this address is different from the subscription address. Try not to confuse the two. Otherwise you may find that you have sent a message to subscribe to all members of the group. Any e-mail messages you send to the list will be sent to all list members unless you address the message to an individual. As with newsgroups, there are certain rules of etiquette that should be followed when posting a message to a mailing list.

Mailing List Etiquette

When corresponding in a mailing list, keep the following rules of etiquette in mind:

- Keep your questions and comments relevant to the focus of the list.
- Remember, what you say is seen by all members of the list. If your reply would have meaning only to the sender of an e-mail message, send your reply to the individual rather than to the list.
- Keep to a minimum the number of lists you subscribe to. The messages from various listservs require extensive system processing and can tie up computer resources. In addition, your mailbox may suddenly become very full.
- When asking a question, you can request that responses be sent to you personally rather than to the list. Then you can compile a summary of the answers to share with the entire list if you want.
- When replying, check that your response is going to the correct location, that is, to the list or the individual.
- When you go on vacation, unsubscribe or suspend mail delivery.

It is possible that a topic you are interested in may have already been discussed, and someone may refer you to a past posting on the list. Many of these past postings are saved (archived) by the listserv. Requesting an information sheet from the listserv will usually provide instructions on how to access archived postings (see command list on page 137).

If you are not interested in the mailing list, send a message back to the subscription address unsubscribing to the list.

Joining a Chat Discussion

Another way to communicate on the Internet is in chat groups.

> **Concept 7: Chat Group**
>
> Communicating in a **chat group** means carrying on a conversation live (in real time) with other people over the Internet. The most common chat system is **Internet relay chat (IRC),** in which users communicate in discussion areas called **channels** or **chat rooms.** There is no restriction to the number of people who can participate in a given discussion, or the number of channels that can be formed over IRC. Before you can talk on IRC, you must have a chat client installed on your computer system. IRC clients have been developed for a variety of computer systems and are available for download from the Internet.
>
> There are also several other types of Web-based, non-IRC chat systems. Although the commands and procedures may differ among them, the underlying principles are the same.
>
> Chatting has been used extensively for live coverage of world events, news, and sports commentary. It also serves as an inexpensive substitute for long distance calling.
>
> Like newsgroups, chat rooms develop their own culture and abbreviations. Some of the commonly used abbreviations and their meanings are listed below.
>
> | Abbreviation | Meaning |
> |---|---|
> | AFK | Away from keyboard |
> | LOL | Laughing out loud |
> | ROTFL | Rolling on the floor laughing |

To demonstrate chatting, you will use the chat group provided by Microsoft.

- Choose Start/Programs/Internet Explorer/Microsoft Chat.

The Chat Connection dialog box on your screen should be similar to Figure 4-14.

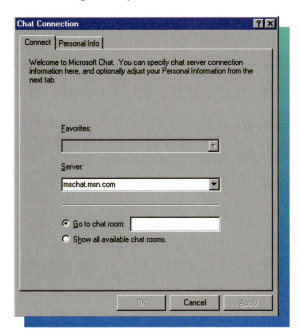

FIGURE 4-14

- Select a server from the drop-down menu or enter the server address provided by your instructor.
- Choose S**h**ow all available chat rooms.
- Click OK .
- If necessary, click OK to close the Message of the Day.

The Chat Room List screen should be similar to Figure 4-15.

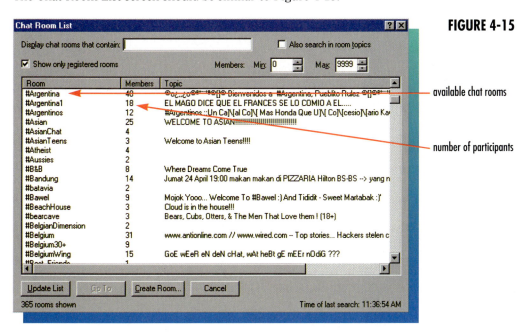

FIGURE 4-15

available chat rooms

number of participants

Once you are connected to a server, you can choose a chat channel. You will be able to select from hundreds of chat channels on many different subjects.

- Select a room of interest to you (#Newbies is a safe site to start chatting).
- Click [Go to].

The chat screen will look similar to Figure 4-16.

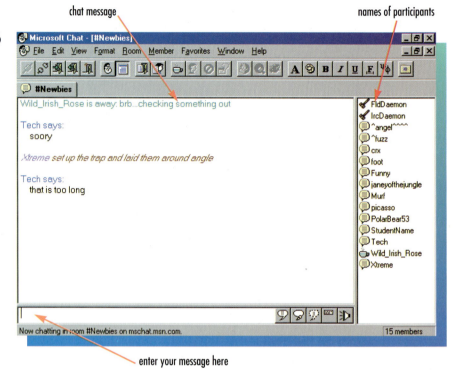

FIGURE 4-16

The left half of the window displays the conversation, and the right lists the names of the users on this chat channel. If this is your first time on a chat channel, you should read the messages being displayed and read the Help files for more information about chatting on the Internet. Once you feel comfortable with chatting, it can be a fun and rewarding experience. There are many options that you can learn how to use to make your chatting fun for you and others. The toolbar buttons display screen tips to help you learn what they are used for.

- Click [icon] to exit the chat group.
- Close all Internet Explorer windows and, if necessary, disconnect from the Internet.

LAB REVIEW

Key Terms

article   (IE118)
Bitnet   (IE133)
channel   (IE140)
chat group   (IE140)
chat room   (IE140)
discussion group   (IE117)
FAQ   (IE126)
flame   (IE126)
flame war   (IE126)
gateway   (IE133)

hierarchy   (IE120)
Internet relay chat (IRC)   (IE140)
list address   (IE135)
listserv address   (IE135)
listserver (listserv)   (IE133)
lurk   (IE126)
mailing list   (IE133)
moderated   (IE118)
newsgroup   (IE118)
newsgroup site   (IE118)

newsreader program   (IE118)
news server   (IE118)
post   (IE118)
subscribe   (IE119)
subscription address   (IE135)
thread   (IE124)
troll   (IE126)
unmoderated   (IE118)
Usenet   (IE118)

Command Summary

Command	Shortcut Key	Button	Action
File/S**e**nd Message	Alt + S		Sends message to discussion group
Go/**N**ews			Opens your news server
Tools/Download t**h**is newsgroup			Displays messages in selected newsgroup
Tools/News**g**roups		News groups	Subscribes to selected newsgroup
Tools/Unsubscr**i**be from this newsgroup			Unsubscribes from selected newsgroup
Compose/**N**ew Message	Ctrl + N	Compose Message	Creates new discussion message
Compose/Reply to Newsgr**o**up	Ctrl + G	Reply to Group	Sends message back to newsgroup
Compose/**C**ancel Message			Removes message you posted to newsgroup

INTERNET EXPLORER 4

Matching

1. Match the following with their definition or function.

1) listserv address _____ **a.** used to separate parts of a newsgroup name
2) unsubscribe _____ **b.** frequently asked questions
3) list address _____ **c.** indicates a follow-up article
4) subscribe _____ **d.** common theme discussions
5) . (dot) _____ **e.** address used to perform mailing list administrative tasks
6) FAQ _____ **f.** a collection of newsgroups
7) post _____ **g.** to remove a newsgroup or mailing list
8) threads _____ **h.** address used to send or post messages to a mailing list
9) Usenet _____ **i.** to add a newsgroup or mailing list
10) Re: _____ **j.** to send a message to a newsgroup or mailing list

Fill-In Questions

1. Using the screen below, enter the correct term for each item.

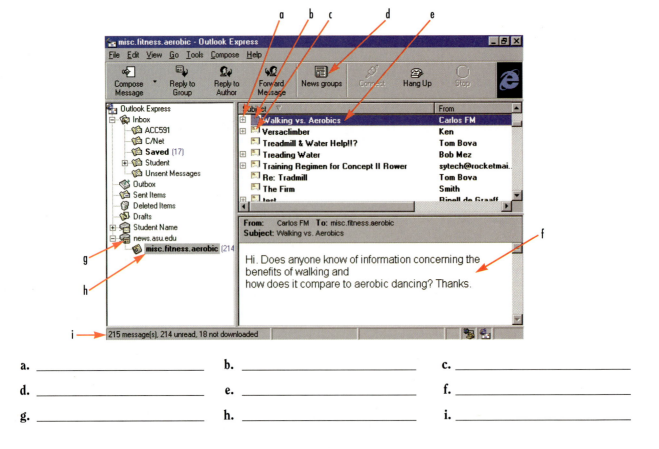

a. _____ b. _____ c. _____
d. _____ e. _____ f. _____
g. _____ h. _____ i. _____

2. Using the screen below, enter the correct term for each item.

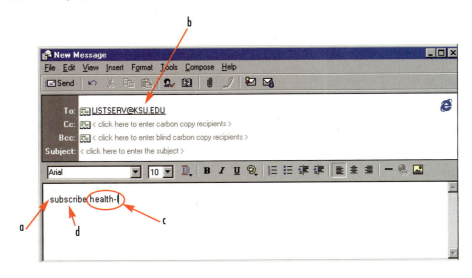

a. _____   b. _____
c. _____   d. _____

Discussion Questions

1. What is a newsgroup? What is a mailing list?
2. What does it mean to subscribe to a newsgroup?
3. What is the difference between a moderated and unmoderated group?
4. What do the parts of newsgroup names separated by dots signify?
5. What different ways can you respond to a newsgroup message?
6. How do you send a new message to a newsgroup?
7. How do you subscribe to a mailing list?
8. Discuss why it is important to follow etiquette when posting messages to newsgroups and mailing lists.

Hands-On Practice Exercises

Step by Step

Rating System
★ Easy
★★ Moderate
★★★ Difficult

1. Find the names of two newsgroups on the topic of computers. Describe the types of messages sent to these groups.

2. Find a newsgroup about the state or country you live in. What is the name of this newsgroup? What types of topics are discussed in this group? Select a topic and describe the types of postings that it contains.

3. Using the list of mailing lists shown in the box on page 149, join a group. Check for messages frequently and remember to unsubscribe or postpone your mail when you are not able to check messages.

4. Locate a newsgroup on a topic that interests you. Read the messages and write a short summary of what types of messages are posted. Discuss how questions and comments are answered and if this group seems to follow the rules of etiquette discussed in the lab.

5. Yahoo has its own chat system. Learn about this chat system at http://www.yahoo.com/. What is different about this chat system? Describe several of its features.

On Your Own

6. Subscribe to a newsgroup of your choice. Read and post messages to it.

7. Try the chat rooms at http://www.acmepet.com for live conversations all about different types of pets.

8. Hot Wired, a popular Web site, has a chat system at http://www.talk.com. Use the <u>Enter</u> link to get on, register, and then follow the procedures to participate in a chat group.

9. Using one of the online mailing list sources (page 149), locate a mailing list on a topic of interest. Subscribe to the list. Check for messages frequently and remember to unsubscribe or postpone your mail when you are not able to check messages.

10. Locate a mailing list and newsgroup that discuss the same issues. Write a brief report on what types of messages are sent to the mailing list and newsgroup. Discuss how the messages are similar and how they are different. Recommend the appropriate list for people with varying interests.

A Newsgroup Sampling

Category	Newsgroup Name	Discussion Area
Business	misc.invest	Investments
	misc.entrepreneurs	Owning your own business
College	alt.college.us	Rumors and reputations of various schools
	soc.college	College activities
Comics	rec.arts.comics.xbooks	X-men comics
	alt.comics.batman	Batman comics
	alt.comics.superman	Superman comics
Dance	rec.art.dance	General dance
Drama	rec.art.theater.plays	Theater and drama
Food and drink	rec.crafts.brewing	Beer brewing
	rec.food.historic	History of food
	alt.food.ice-cream	Ice cream
	alt.religion.santaism	Santa Claus
Fun	rec.rollercoaster	Fans of roller coasters exchange experiences
Games	alt.atari-jaguar.discussion	Video games
	rec.games.video.nintendo	Nintendo video games
Government	clari.news.usa.gov.white_house	White House news
Health	alt.support.diet	Dieting support
	clari.tw.health	Health care and medicine
Hobbies	rec.radio.amateur.equipment	Equipment for amateur radios
	rec.antiques	Buy, sell, and trade antiques
	rec.juggling	Juggling oranges, numbers, etc.
	rec.crafts.quilting	Quilting
Home	alt.home.repair	Home repair
	alt.hoovers	Vacuum cleaners
Humor	alt.humor.puns	Word play
Jobs	bionet.jobs.wanted	Biological sciences jobs
	misc.jobs.offered.entry	Entry-level jobs
	misc.jobs.resumes	Posted resumes
Medicine	alt.med.allergy	Causes and treatments for allergies
	sci.med.dentistry	Dentistry
Music	rec.music.classical	Classical music
	rec.music.marketplace	Buy or sell musical instruments, equipment, records, etc.
	rec.music.compose	Compose original music

A Newsgroup Sampling (concluded)

Category	Newsgroup Name	Discussion Area
Pets	alt.aquaria	Tropical fish
	rec.equestrian	Horse lovers
	rec.pets.birds	Advice and anecdotes on birds
	rec.pets.cats	Advice and anecdotes on cats
	rec.pets.dogs	Advice and anecdotes on dogs
Science	sci.astro.planetarium	Planetarium programs
	bionet.cellbiol	Cell biology
	alt.energy.renewable	Renewable energy
Travel	rec.travel.france	Travel information on France
	rec.travel.air	Deals on air tickets and other bargains
	rec.travel.marketplace	Deals on air tickets and other bargains

A Mailing List Sampling

Topic	Subscription Address (listserv@)	List Name
ER (television show)	gcp.thenorth.com	er-l
Jag (television show)	american.edu	jagtv-l
College Bowl discussion	listserv.rice.edu	cb-l
Ceramic arts	lsv.uky.edu	clayart
Theatre and musical artists	lists.psu.edu	collab-l
D+D cartoons	netspace.org	d+d-cartoon
Earthsave	discussiomaelstrom.stjohns.edu	earthsave
Sharks and cartilaginous fish	raven.utc.edu	shark-l
Rare books	listserv.indiana.edu	rarebook-l
Books by Anne Rice	lists.psu.edu	arbooks
Sociology and computers	discussiovm.temple.edu	asascan
Use of computers in sport	listserv.unb.ca	sportpc
Advanced manufacturing methods	vm.its.rpi.edu	amm-l
Computer-aided design and manufacturing	listserv.syr.edu	cadam-l
Movie poster discussion	american.edu	mopo-l
Internet in business	listserv.aol.com	inbusiness
Internet and Computer Law Association	lists.ufl.edu	intlaw-l
Food and wine	cmuvm.csv.cmich.edu	foodwine
Exercise and sports psychology	vm.temple.edu	sportpsy
Women in Sports and Physical Activity Journal	listserv.uta.edu	wspaj-l
Exercise/diet/wellness	etsuadmn.bitnet	fit-l

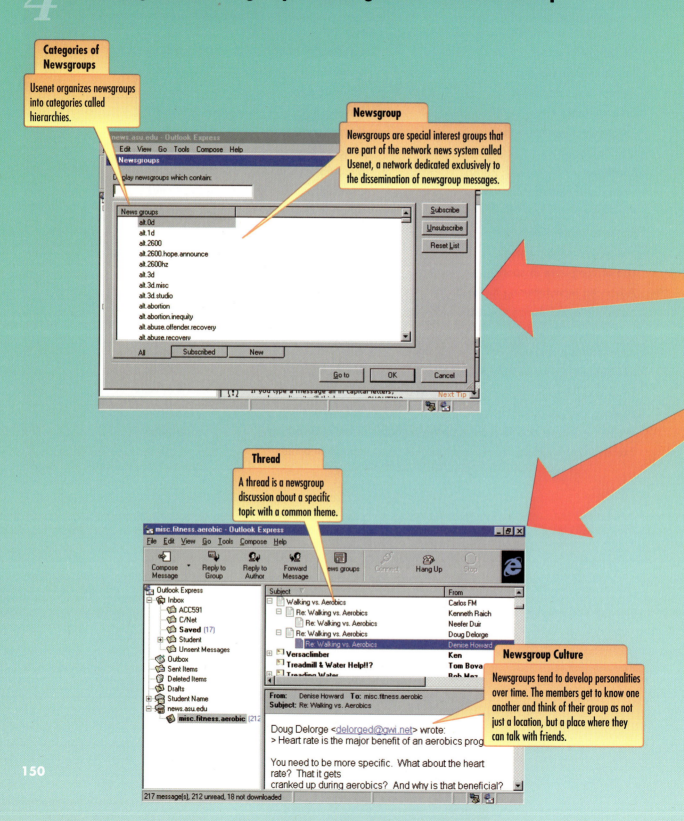

Mailing List

Mailing lists consist of the e-mail addresses of a group of people who have subscribed to the mailing list because they are interested in the topic of the group.

Subscription Address and List Address

The subscription address is used to perform administrative tasks with the listserver, and the list address is used to communicate with mailing list members.

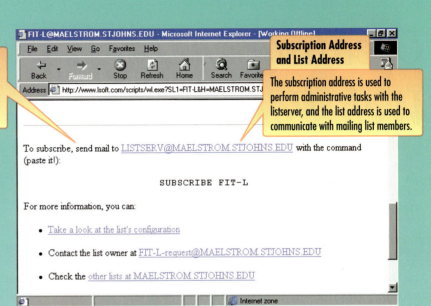

Concepts

- Newsgroup
  Categories of Newsgroups
- Thread
  Newsgroup Culture
- Mailing List
  Subscription Address and List Address
- Chat Group

Chat Group

Communicating in a chat group means carrying on a conversation live (in real time) with other people over the Internet.

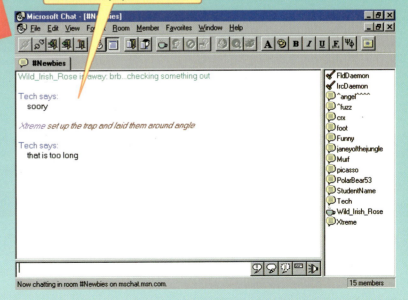

Creating Web Pages

COMPETENCIES

After completing this lab, you will know how to:

1. Design a Web page.
2. Enter the page content.
3. Format text.
4. Align paragraphs.
5. Apply character effects.
6. Add a background.
7. Insert images.
8. Preview a Web page.
9. Add lines.
10. Create a bulleted list.
11. Create links.
12. Publish a Web page.

CASE STUDY

You have met with the Web site administrator and discussed the steps you need to take to create the new Web page of related links to the newsletter articles. Your next step is to convert the text document of links to a Web page. Web pages can take minutes to hours to create, depending upon the complexity of the page design. This lab will discuss some of the fundamentals of designing and creating a Web page using Internet Explorer's FrontPage Express.

You have been asked to develop an overall design and layout for the new Web page. Your completed Web page will look like that shown below.

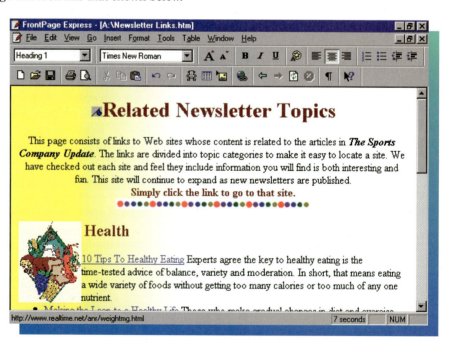

Concept Overview

The following concepts will be introduced in this lab:

1. Web Page Design	Many elements can be added to a Web page to make it attractive and easy to use. Graphic objects, images, art, and color are perhaps the most important features of Web pages.
2. HTML Tags	HTML tags are embedded codes that supply information about the page's structure, appearance, and contents.
3. Font	A font, also commonly referred to as a typeface, is a set of characters with a specific design.
4. Paragraph Alignment	Alignment is how text is positioned on a line between the margins or indents. There are three types of paragraph alignment: left, center, and right.
5. Character Effects	Different character effects such as bold, italics, and color can be applied to selections to add emphasis or interest to a page.
6. Images	Authors use images in Web pages to provide information or decoration, or to communicate their personal or organization's style.
7. Absolute and Relative Links	When you create a hyperlink in a Web page, you can make the path to the destination of the hyperlink an absolute link or a relative link.

Designing a Web Page

You have discussed the purpose of the new Web page with Donna Blackcloud, the site administrator. She suggested that you create the new Web page of related links using Microsoft FrontPage Express 2 that is included with Internet Explorer.

- Choose Start/**P**rograms/Internet Explorer/FrontPage Express.
- If necessary, maximize the window.

> Your instructor will provide you with the correct location if it is different from the one provided in this text.

Your screen should be similar to Figure 5-1.

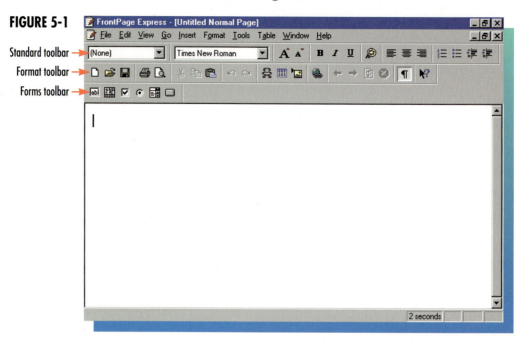

FIGURE 5-1

The FrontPage Express window includes menus, commands, and options that provide the tools you will need to create a Web page. In addition, it includes a Standard toolbar, Format toolbar, and Forms toolbar, which contain shortcuts for many of the menu options. The View menu is used to show or hide the toolbars.

- If necessary, use the View menu to display the Standard and Format toolbars and to hide the Forms toolbar.

When creating or **authoring** a Web page, you want to make the page both attractive and informative. You also want it to be easy to use and to work right. It is important, therefore, to plan the design of the Web site and the pages it will include in advance.

Concept 1: Web Page Design

Many elements can be added to a Web page to make it attractive and easy to use. Graphic objects, images, art, and color are perhaps the most important features of Web pages. They entice the user to continue to explore the Web site. Other elements, such as animations, scrolling banners, blinking text, audio, and video can be added to a Web page to make it even more dynamic. With all these elements, it is easy to add too many to a page and end up with a cluttered and distracting mess. Keep the following design tips in mind when authoring your own Web pages.

- The text content of your page is the single most important element. Text should be readable against the background. Check for proper spelling and grammar.

- Background colors and patterns add interest and pizzazz to a page, but be careful that they do not make the page hard to read. Additionally, keep in mind that more complex patterns take longer to download. Also, since many users have 256-color monitors, higher resolution colors will be lost and may not look good on their monitors.

- Keep graphics and animations simple to speed up downloading, and avoid busy animations and blinking text. A good suggestion is to keep images less than 100K in file size. Smaller is even better.

- Page dimensions should be the same as the browser window size. Because many users have their screen resolution set to 640 by 480 pixels, designing a page for 600 by 800 pixels will be too large for their screens.

- In general, keep your page length no longer than two to three screens' worth of information. If a page is too long, the reader has to remember too much information that has scrolled off the screen.

- At the bottom of each page, include navigation links back to the home page and other major site pages so users will not get lost. Also include text links for users who have turned off graphics loading in their browsers to improve downloading speed.

- Because not all browsers support all HTML features, do not make your document overly dependent on HTML features that cannot be seen by all browsers. For example, some browsers might not accept your graphics or animations, in which case you would want to provide alternative text.

- Although frames can make navigation in your Web site easier, too many can make it difficult to read the screen. Use the minimum number of frames possible. Many browsers cannot display frames, so you may want to consider creating a non-frame version to accommodate those users.

- Get permission before using text, sounds, and images that are copyrighted. Copyright laws and infringement fines apply to pages posted on the Internet.

The site administrator suggested using the same basic layout and colors that are used in other pages in the site to maintain a unified look. In addition, since the site will be mostly text links, she suggested that you include graphic images and animations to make the site more interesting to view. After considering these features, you drew a sample page layout that you feel may be both interesting and easy to use.

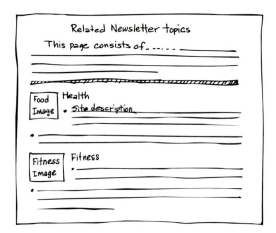

Entering the Page Content

As you learned in Lab 1, all pages on the WWW are written using a programming language called HTML (Hypertext Markup Language). Every item on a Web page has properties associated with it that are encoded in HTML tags.

Concept 2: HTML Tags

HTML **tags** are embedded codes that supply information about the page's structure, appearance, and contents. They tell your browser where the title, heading, paragraphs, images, links, bold text, listings, and other information are to appear on the page. In addition, they designate links to other Web pages. Tags usually appear on either side of the selected text and consist of two parts. The first part tells where to begin the feature and the second part tells where to end it. A slash (/) in the ending tag means "end command." All tags are surrounded by the less-than and greater-than symbols (<>). Only the selected text appears in the format specified by the tag. Tags do not show when you load the HTML page on your browser. Examples of some simple tags and their effects are shown below.

Tagged text	Effect
<B> Hello </B>	Bolds the word **Hello**
<P> text </P>	Marks the beginning and end of a paragraph
<TITLE>The Sports Company</TITLE>	Displays text as a title

All Web pages commonly include a title, different levels of headings, and text design elements such as horizontal rules. Each of these elements has its own tag.

FrontPage Express is an authoring tool that lets you create a Web page without needing to know the HTML codes. It makes it easy to create and design a page by generating the HTML tags automatically while you are using many of the same features you would use in a word processor to create a text document.

FrontPage Express offers several ways to create Web pages. You can edit a Web page you are viewing in the Internet Explorer window or a page you have saved as an HTML file on your disk. You can also use one of the wizards or templates to help you quickly create a Web page. A wizard provides step-by-step directions to help you create a Web page. You complete each step by entering text and adding elements such as lines and bullets. When you have completed the steps, you have the basics for a page that you can further refine using the FrontPage Express window. Finally, you can start from scratch with a blank Web page.

> Use **F**ile/**N**ew or Ctrl + N to access the wizards or templates.

You have already entered the text for the Web page in a FrontPage Express document.

- Open the file Related Links.htm from your data disk.

> Click 📂 or use **F**ile/**O**pen to open an existing file.

Your screen should be similar to Figure 5-2.

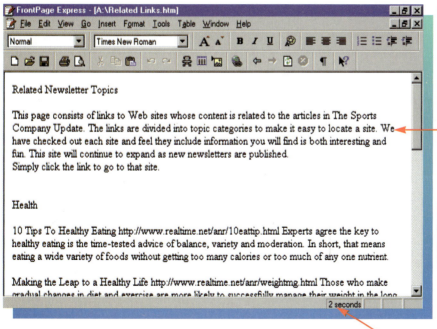

FIGURE 5-2

text for Web page

estimated download time

> If necessary, click ¶ or use **V**iew/Format **M**arks to turn off the display of formatting symbols.

So far this page looks like any other text document. However, FrontPage Express included the necessary HTML tags. To see the HTML code,

- Choose **V**iew/**H**TML.

> FrontPage Express estimates the page's download time in seconds at 28,800 kbps.

Your screen should be similar to Figure 5-3.

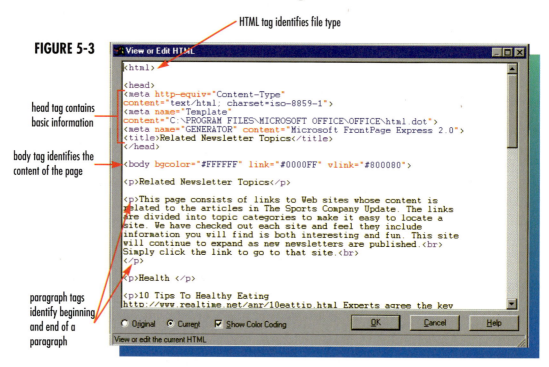

FIGURE 5-3

A second window is open that displays the contents of the page and its HTML coding. All HTML document files begin with the <html> tag, which tells the browser that the document it is reading is an HTML document. They also contain a <head> tag, which includes basic information needed by the browser, and a <body> tag, which indicates the area where the body of the page will appear. Each paragraph begins and ends with a <p> (paragraph) tag.

■ Click **OK** to close this window.

Now that the content of the page is complete, you are ready to enhance the appearance of the page.

Formatting Text

FrontPage Express includes two types of format styles, paragraph and character. Paragraph formats consist of combinations of formats that affect all paragraphs in the selection or the paragraph in which the insertion point is located. Character formats are formats such as font types, styles, sizes, and colors that affect the selected text only. When text is first entered in a blank HTML document, it is formatted using the default paragraph style of Normal. This sets the font type to New Times Roman and the font size to 12 points.

Concept 3: Font

A **font,** also commonly referred to as a **typeface,** is a set of characters with a specific design. The designs have names such as Times New Roman and Courier New. Using fonts as a design element can add interest to your page and give readers visual cues to help them find information quickly. It is good practice to use only two types of fonts in a document, one for text and one for headers. Too many font styles can make your document look cluttered and unprofessional.

Some fonts, such as Courier New, are **fixed font,** which means that each character takes up the same amount of space. Most fonts are **variable font,** which means that some letters, such as m or w, take up more space than other letters, such as i or t. Arial and Times New Roman are variable fonts.

Each font has one or more sizes. Size is the height and width of the character and is commonly measured in **points,** abbreviated "pt." One point equals about 1/72 inch, and text in most documents is 10 pt. or 12 pt.

Several common fonts in different sizes are shown in the following table.

Font Name	Font Size
Arial	This is 10 pt. This is 16 pt.
Courier New	This is 10 pt. This is 16 pt.
Times New Roman	This is 10 pt. This is 16 pt.

HTML converts point sizes to the closest HTML size, a range from 1 to 7 (8 to 36 pt.). The HTML range instructs the browser to display the text within the tag in the specified HTML size. The font may not appear in the specified size if the browser's font preferences are different.

First you will change the page title to the Heading paragraph style. Headings make it easier to locate information on a page by visually dividing it into sections. The six heading levels differ from normal text by their type size. The most important heading on your page should be assigned a Heading 1 level, the next most important a Heading 2 level, and so on.

- Click on the page title.
- Click [Normal ▼] to open the Change Style drop-down list.
- Click Heading 1.

> The menu equivalent is F**o**rmat/**P**aragraph.

> You could also click [A⁺] to incrementally increase text size and [A⁻] to decrease it.

Your screen should be similar to Figure 5-4.

FIGURE 5-4

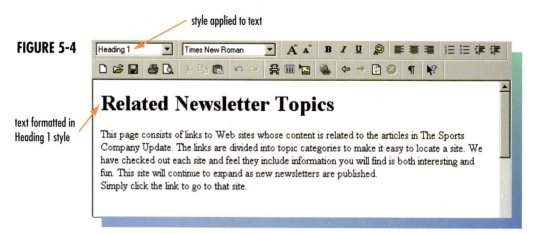

style applied to text

text formatted in Heading 1 style

Aligning Paragraphs

Next you want to change the alignment of the page title so it is centered on the page.

Concept 4: Paragraph Alignment

Alignment is how text is positioned on a line between the margins or indents. There are three types of paragraph alignment: left, center, and right.

Alignment		Effect on Text
Left		Aligns text against the left margin of the page, leaving the right margin ragged. This is the most commonly used paragraph alignment type and therefore the default setting.
Center		Centers each line of text between left and right margins. Center alignment is used mostly for headings or centering graphics on a page.
Right		Aligns text against right margin, leaving left margin ragged. Use right alignment when you want text to line up on the outside of a page, such as a chapter title or a header.

The menu equivalent is F**o**rmat/**P**aragraph/Paragraph **A**lignment/Center.

- If necessary, move the insertion point to the page title.
- Click ▤ Center.

The title is now centered on the line between the left and right margins.

Applying Character Effects

You also want to add color to the page title. Color is one of several character effects that can be used to enhance the appearance of text in a Web page.

Concept 5: Character Effects

Different character effects such as bold, italics, and color can be applied to selections to add emphasis or interest to a page. The table below describes the effects and their uses.

Format	Example	Use
Bold	**Bold**	Adds emphasis
Italic	*Italic*	Adds emphasis
Underline	Underline	Adds emphasis
Superscript	"To be or not to be."[1]	Used in footnotes and formulas
Subscript	H_2O	Used in formulas
Non-breaking	Text does not wrap	Used when you do not want text to wrap to window width
Blink	Text blinks on/off	Adds interest
Color	Color Color Color	Adds interest

- Select the entire page title.
- Click Text Color.
- Select a dark red color.
- Click OK.
- Click on the title to clear the selection.

> You must highlight the text you want the character effects applied to.
>
> Click in the margin to the left of the line or drag to select the text.
>
> The menu equivalent is F<u>o</u>rmat/<u>F</u>ont/<u>C</u>olor.

Your screen should be similar to Figure 5-5.

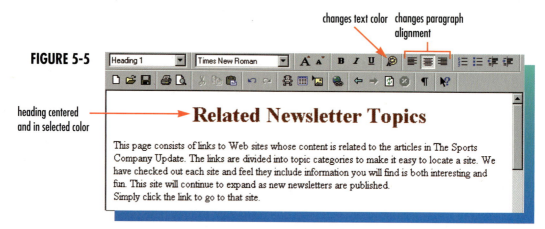

FIGURE 5-5

heading centered and in selected color

The title now looks much more impressive. Because the insertion point is positioned on the title, the style and alignment buttons reflect the settings applied to the title.

You also want to improve the appearance of the introductory paragraphs by centering them, and to add italics and bold to the newsletter name.

- Move the insertion point to anywhere in the introductory paragraph and center it.
- Select the newsletter title, The Sports Company Update.
- Click **B** Bold.
- Click *I* Italic.
- Add bold and the same dark red color as the title to the last sentence of the introductory paragraph.

Next you want to apply heading styles and color to the category heads Health and Fitness. Since these are the next most important headings on the page, you will apply a Heading 2 level.

- Move the insertion point to anywhere in the Health heading and apply a Heading 2 level.
- Select the Health heading and change the characters to the same dark red color as the title.
- Apply a Heading 2 level and the same color to the Fitness heading.
- Move to the top of the page.

> The menu equivalent is Format/Font/Font Style/Bold Italic.

> Double-click a word to select it.

> Scroll the page to see the Fitness heading.

Your screen should be similar to Figure 5-6.

FIGURE 5-6

Adding a Background

So far your page is very plain and contains a lot of text. You still want to make several changes to improve the appearance of the page. One of the quickest changes you can make to enhance the appearance of the Web page is to change the background. A **background** is a color or design that is displayed behind the text on the page. You can change the background to another color or select a background image, pattern, or texture, called a **wallpaper.** To add a background,

■ Choose Format/Background.

> Any picture image that has a bitmap file type (.bmp) can be converted for use as wallpaper.

The Page Properties dialog box on your screen should be similar to Figure 5-7.

FIGURE 5-7

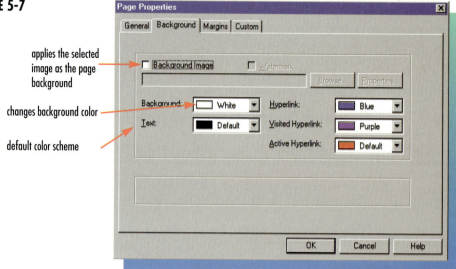

This dialog box allows you to modify the text color of regular text as well as hyperlink text and apply a background color or image to the Web page. The current settings are Internet Explorer's default color scheme page settings. To try a different background color,

- Open the Background drop-down menu and select a color of your choice.
- Click OK.

Your screen should be similar to Figure 5-8.

FIGURE 5-8

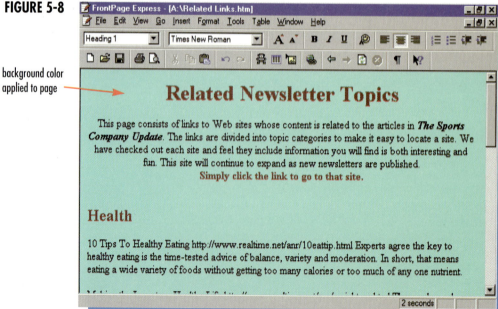

The color you selected is applied to the page. Next you will try a background image instead. The image you will use for your wallpaper is on your data disk.

- Choose Format/Background.
- Select Background Image.
- Click Browse (twice).
- From the Select Background Image dialog box, set the Look In location to the drive containing your data disk.
- Select Yellowgrade.gif.
- Click Open.
- Click OK.

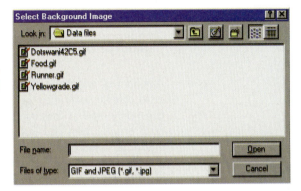

The background image you selected overlays much of the background color of your selected color scheme.

- Return the background color to white.

Your screen should be similar to Figure 5-9.

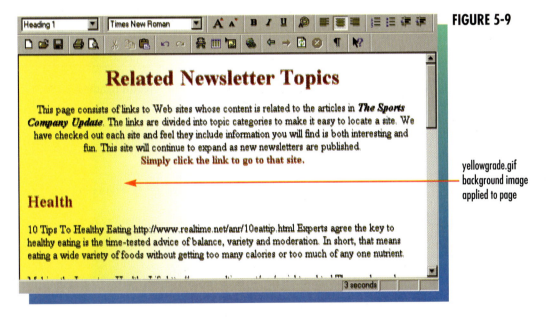

FIGURE 5-9

yellowgrade.gif background image applied to page

When applying a background, be sure there is enough contrast between the background and the text so that the page is easy to read.

Inserting Images

Next to each of the category heads, you want to display the same pictures that are in the newsletter. Picture images and other types of graphic objects are one of the most important features of the Web pages.

> **Concept 6: Images**
>
> Authors use images in Web pages to provide information or decoration, or to communicate their personal or organization's style. They are also commonly used to display graphic artwork or pictures of products for sale. Each graphic item you insert in an HTML file is stored in a separate file that is accessed and loaded by the browser at the same time as the page is loaded. FrontPage Express creates a link to the object's file in the HTML file. The link is a tag that includes the location and file name of the object the browser is to load and display in the page.
>
> Graphic objects are commonly inserted into HTML documents in GIF and JPEG file formats. If you insert an image that is not in either of these formats, the image will be saved in the GIF format when the file is saved.
>
> Another feature associated with graphic objects is how text aligns with the object or wraps around it. You can specify whether to have the image right-align or left-align to the page. You can also specify the particular sides you want the text to wrap to and the distance between the object and the text that surrounds it.

First you will add the picture of food before the Health heading.

- Move to the beginning of the word "Health."
- Click [icon] Insert Image.
- Open the Other Location tab.

> The menu equivalent is **I**nsert/**I**mage.

The Image dialog box on your screen should be similar to Figure 5-10.

FIGURE 5-10

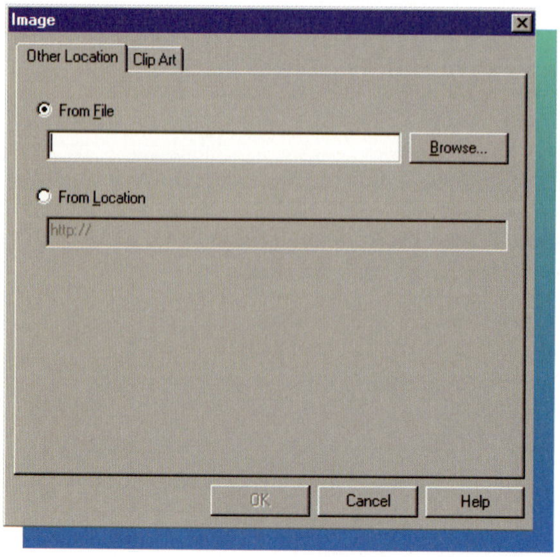

This dialog box is used to insert a new image. To specify a picture image to insert,

- Click **Browse...**.
- Change the location to your data disk and select the picture file Food.gif.
- Click **Open**.

The picture is inserted, but it is much too large and you would like to reduce its size. To do this you must first select the object.

- Click on the food picture.

Your screen should be similar to Figure 5-11.

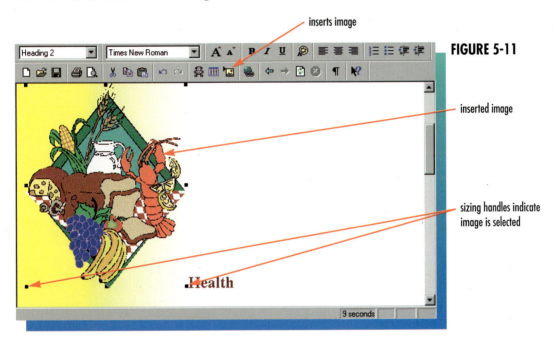

FIGURE 5-11

The picture is surrounded by eight boxes called **sizing handles.** They indicate the graphic is selected and can now be sized and moved. A graphic object is sized much like you size a window. You want to reduce the image to approximately 1.5 inches wide by 2 inches high.

- Point to the lower right corner handle.
- When the mouse pointer is ⤡, drag the mouse inward to reduce the size of the picture to approximately 1.5 by 2 inches. (See Figure 5-12.)

> Drag the corner handle to maintain the picture proportions.

Your screen should be similar to Figure 5-12.

FIGURE 5-12

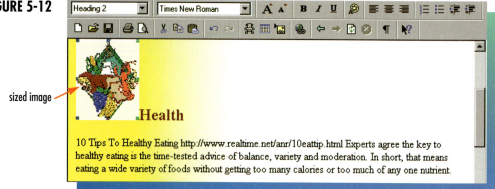

You also want to change how the text wraps around the image.

- Right-click the image and select Image Properties from the shortcut menu.
- Open the Appearance tab.

> The menu equivalent is Edit/Image Properties, and the keyboard shortcut is Alt + Enter.

Your screen should be similar to Figure 5-13.

FIGURE 5-13

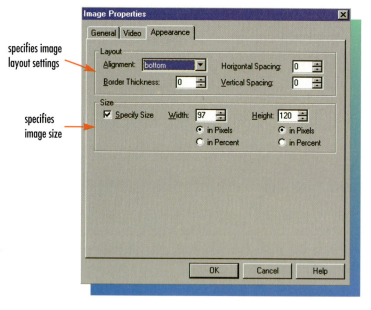

Features in the Appearance tab modify an image's properties, such as how text aligns with the image, the spacing between the image and text, and the size of the image.

> You can precisely size an image by setting the height and width values.

- Choose Left from the Alignment drop-down list.
- Click OK.

The image remains aligned with the left margin and the text wraps to the right side of the image.

- In a similar manner, insert the image Runner.gif before the Fitness heading. Wrap the text to the right side of the image and size it as in Figure 5-14.

Your screen should be similar to Figure 5-14.

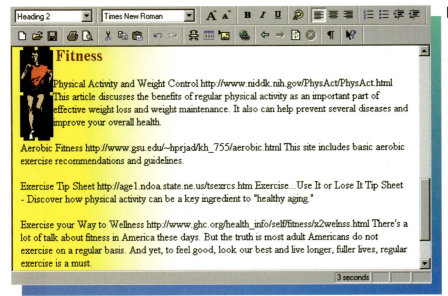

FIGURE 5-14

Previewing the Page

Next you want to see how the page will look when viewed in the Internet Explorer window. Before viewing the file in Internet Explorer, you need to save the file.

- Choose **F**ile/Save **A**s.

First you need to enter a title for the page. Each page includes a title that is displayed in the browser window title bar when the page is displayed. The information in the title is

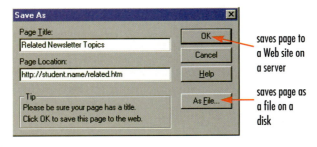

used by most Web search tools to locate specific Web pages. It is also used as the page's title for the Favorites list. You will replace the current title with a more descriptive one.

- Enter the page title of **Health and Fitness Links.**

Creating Web Pages

Then, to save this page as a file on your data disk,

- Click **As File...**.
- Enter the file name of **Newsletter Links.**
- Click **Save**.

> You can also save the page to a Web site on a server by clicking **OK**.

To see how your page will look when displayed in the Internet Explorer window,

- Start Internet Explorer.
- If your computer displays the screen to access your Internet provider, enter the requested user identification.
- Choose **F**ile/**O**pen.
- Click **Browse...**.
- Change the location to your data disk and select the Newsletter Links.htm file
- Click **Open**.
- Click **OK**.

> Use the Start menu or use  in the Quick Launch toolbar to start Explorer.

Your screen should be similar to Figure 5-15.

FIGURE 5-15

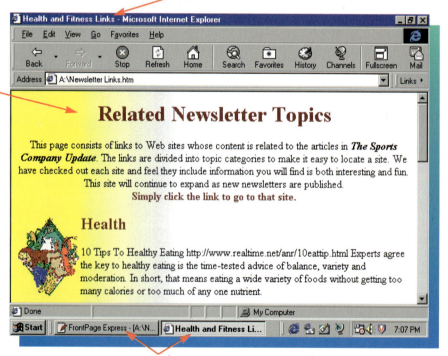

page title appears in title bar

Web page displayed in Internet Explorer browser window

two open applications

The page is displayed in the Internet Explorer window and you can now see how the page will appear when displayed by a browser. The FrontPage Express window is still open behind the Internet Explorer window.

> The taskbar displays two task buttons, one for each open application.

- Scroll the page to see the Fitness area.

The page is much more interesting with the addition of the graphics. However, you still want to add lines, bullets, and other enhancements to improve its appearance.

- Return to the top of the page.

Adding Lines

Next you want to separate the introductory paragraph from the Health section of the page with a horizontal line.

- Switch back to the FrontPage Express window.
- Move to the blank line above the Health heading.
- Choose Insert/Horizontal Line.

> Click [FrontPage Express] in the taskbar.

The standard horizontal line consists of a simple gray line that extends the width of the window. You decide this is not very interesting and instead want to insert a moving graphic line. A common source of graphic images is called **Clip Art.** These images consist of simple drawings that are commonly included with an application program. To delete the line and insert another,

> You can also modify the properties, such as line width and color, of the standard horizontal line.

- Click [icon] Undo.
- Click [icon] Insert Image.
- Open the Clip Art tab.
- Select the Animations category from the Category drop-down list.

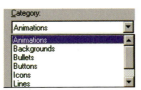

> You can also purchase Clip Art packages to add to your collection.

> You could also select the graphic line and press Del.

> The Lines category includes many graphic horizontal line options.

The Image dialog box on your screen should be similar to Figure 5-16.

FIGURE 5-16

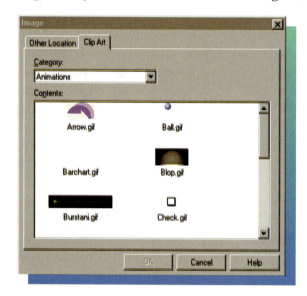

> If the Clip Art file Dotswani.gif is not listed in the Animations category, open the Other Location tab and select it from your data disk.

- Select the Dotswani.gif file.
- Click **OK**.

Your screen should be similar to Figure 5-17.

FIGURE 5-17

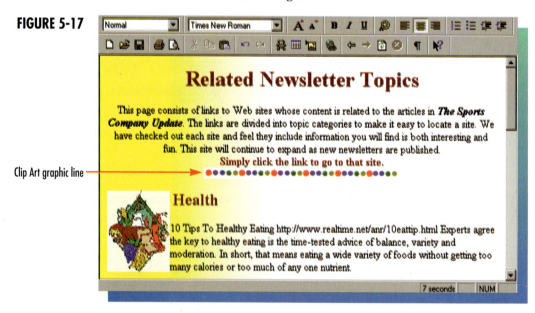

Clip Art graphic line

The Clip Art graphic line adds interest and, as you will see, animation to the page. To see it moving, you need to view the page in the browser window.

> The menu equivalent is <u>F</u>ile/<u>S</u>ave, and the keyboard shortcut is Ctrl + S.

- Click 💾 Save to save the file again.
- Click **Yes** to save the image to a file.

- Switch to the Internet Explorer window.
- Click [Refresh].
- Switch back to the FrontPage Express window.

Creating a Bulleted List

Next you want to add bullets to the beginning of each Web site description in the list.

- Move to the first site description under Health.
- Click [≡] Bulleted List.

> The menu equivalent is F**o**rmat/Bullets and **N**umbering.

Although not visible, a bullet has been added to the first line of the description. It is not visible because it is hidden by the graphic. It will, however, display correctly when you view the page in the browser.

> You could also choose Bulleted List from the Change Style drop-down list.

- Add a bullet to the second site description.

Your screen should be similar to Figure 5-18.

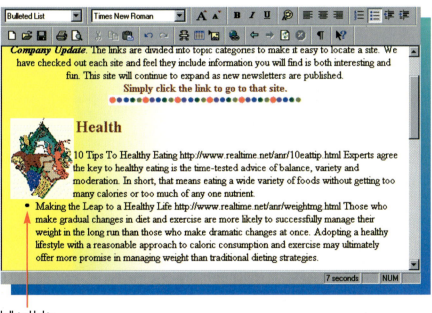

FIGURE 5-18

bullet added to paragraph

Now you can see the bullet. Adding a bullet also indents the entire paragraph and removes the blank line between each bulleted list item.

> If necessary, scroll the window to refresh the display.

- Add bullets to each of the remaining site descriptions.

To see the changes you have made in the browser window,

- Click ![save] Save to save the file again.
- Switch to the Internet Explorer window.
- Click ![refresh].

Your screen should be similar to Figure 5-19.

FIGURE 5-19

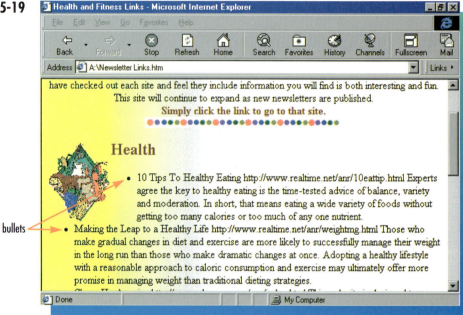

bullets

Creating Links

Next you want to convert the site references to hyperlinks so the reader can quickly jump to the associated site. There are two types of hyperlinks, absolute and relative.

Concept 7: Absolute and Relative Hyperlinks

When you create a hyperlink in a Web page, you can make the path to the destination of the hyperlink an absolute link or a relative link. An **absolute link,** also called a **fixed link,** is a link that identifies the file location of the destination by its full address, such as c:\Word Data File\Sales.doc. A **relative link** identifies the destination location in relation to the location of the Web page file. A relative link is based on a path you specify in which the first part of the path is shared by both the Web page file that contains the hyperlink and the destination file.

A relative link changes when the Web page file is moved to another location. It is used to make it easy to copy materials to another location, which is needed, for example, when you upload your Web pages to a server. A fixed link will not change, regardless if you move the Web page file to another location. Fixed links are usually only used if you are sure the location of the destination file will not change. Hyperlinks to documents on other Web sites are called **external links** and should typically use a fixed file location that includes the URL of the page.

Creating Links   IE175

You will change the name of each site to a hyperlink. Since the sites are external links, they require the use of an absolute link address. You will use the URL in each description to create the link.

- Display the FrontPage Express window.
- Select the URL following the text "10 Tips To Healthy Eating" in the first site description.
- Click ✂ Cut to remove it from the page and store it in the Clipboard.
- Select the text "10 Tips To Healthy Eating."
- Click 🔗 Create Hyperlink.

> The menu equivalent is Insert/Hyperlink, and the keyboard shortcut is Ctrl + K.

The Create Hyperlink dialog box on your screen should be similar to Figure 5-20.

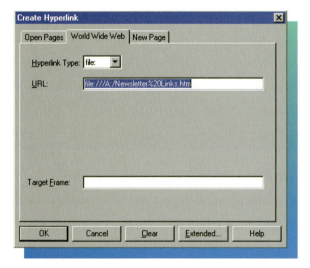

FIGURE 5-20

In the dialog box you enter the URL for the link you are creating. To paste the URL from the Clipboard into the URL text box, you will need to use the keyboard shortcut for the Paste command.

- Press Ctrl + V.
- Click OK.
- Click the page to clear the selection.

INTERNET EXPLORER 4

Your screen should be similar to Figure 5-21.

FIGURE 5-21

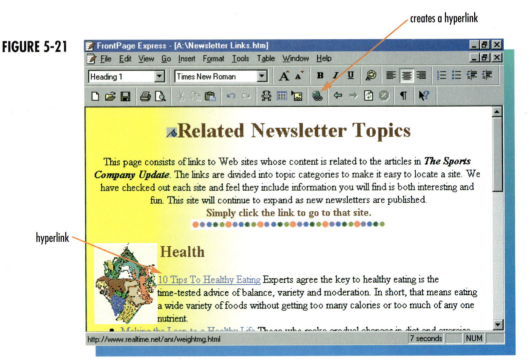

The selected text appears formatted as a hyperlink.

- In the same manner, cut the URLs for each description and create a hyperlink to the description title.
- View your changes in the Internet Explorer window.

This page should also include links to other pages within The Sports Company Web site. Because you do not know the locations of those pages, you will leave it to the Web site administrator to add those links. However, you do want to include a link at the bottom of the page to quickly return to the top of the page. To do this you create a **bookmark** or **anchor** in the Web page and then create a link that points to the bookmark. When you click on the link, the browser jumps to the bookmark location. First you will create the bookmark.

- Switch to the FrontPage Express window.
- Move the insertion point to the beginning of the page title.
- Choose Edit/Bookmark.
- Enter the name **Top of page** for the bookmark in the Bookmark Name text box.
- Click OK.

> You can also create a hyperlink without selecting the text first. The URL is inserted as the link text. You can then edit the link to display whatever text you want.

> Use Edit/Unlink to remove a hyperlink.

> You can also drag and drop objects from your desktop or other Web pages onto your Web page to create a link to the object.

> You can also turn an image into a hyperlink in the same way: select the image and click.

Your screen should be similar to Figure 5-22.

icon marks location of bookmark

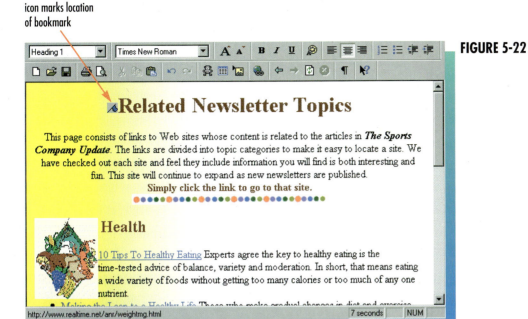

FIGURE 5-22

A special icon appears in the document to mark the location of the bookmark. Next you need to enter the text for the link at the bottom of the page and create the link to the bookmark.

- Enter the text **Top of Page** at the bottom of the page.
- Press ⏎Enter.
- Select the Top of Page text.
- Click 🔗 Create Hyperlink.
- Open the Open Pages tab.

The Create Hyperlinks dialog box on your screen should be similar to Figure 5-23.

currently open Web page in FrontPage Express

displays bookmark in the selected open page

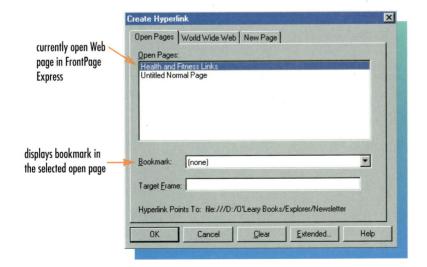

FIGURE 5-23

Creating Web Pages

The Open Pages tab lists the names of all open Web pages in FrontPage Express and is used to specify the bookmark location. Next you will select the bookmark as the location to link to and see if your link works correctly.

- Open the Bookmark drop-down menu.
- Select Top of page.
- Click OK.
- Save the page and view it in the browser window.
- Scroll to the bottom of the page and click Top of Page.

> The Bookmark drop-down menu lists the names of all bookmarks in the selected page.

The top of the page where the anchor is located is displayed in the window. Next you will check the other links.

- Click 10 Tips to Healthy Eating.

Internet Explorer locates the Web page, loads it, and displays it in the window. Your screen should be similar to Figure 5-24.

FIGURE 5-24

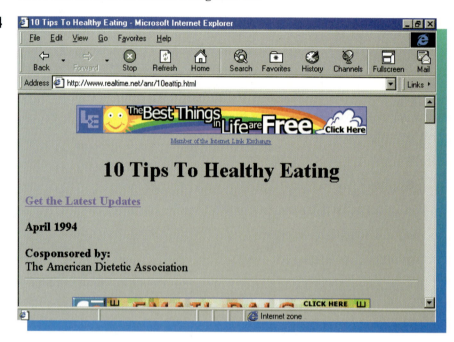

To return to the Health and Fitness Links page,

- Click Back.
- Close the Internet Explorer window and disconnect from the Internet.

Your Web page should be displayed in the FrontPage Express window.

- Display the HTML source code.

Your screen should be similar to Figure 5-25.

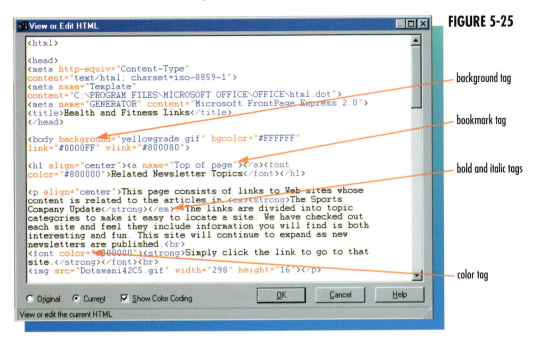

FIGURE 5-25

— background tag
— bookmark tag
— bold and italic tags
— color tag

- Scroll the window to see the entire HTML file.

As you can see, many more HTML tags have been added to the file.

- Close the View or Edit HTML window.
- Add your name and the current date on a single line at the bottom of the Web page.
- Save and print the page.
- Exit FrontPage Express.

Click 🖨 or use **F**ile/**P**rint or Ctrl + P to print the page.

Click ✕ in the title bar or use **F**ile/**E**xit to exit the program.

Publishing a Web Page

The process of placing your Web pages on a server for public access by others is commonly referred to as **publishing.** Before making your Web page public, however, you should test that all links work correctly. In addition, because all browsers do not display the HTML tags the same way, it is a good idea to preview your page using different browsers. Many of the differences in the way browsers display a page are appearance differences, not structural.

How do you get your page on the Internet so others can see it? The steps that you take to make your pages available to other people depend on how you want to share them. There are two main avenues: on your local network or intranet server for limited access by people within an organization, or on an Internet server for access by anyone using the WWW. In either case, you need to upload your Web page files and all related files, such as pictures and Clip Art image files, to a remote server. If you do not include all the files, your links will not work. You should ask the Web administrator how the Web pages, graphics files, and other files should be structured on the server. For instance, find out

> Refer to the Appendix for more information on FTP.

> To make your Web pages available on the WWW, you need to either install Web server software on your computer or locate an Internet service provider that allocates space for Web pages.

whether you need to create separate folders for bullets and pictures, or whether you need to store all the files in one location. If you plan to use forms or image maps, you should ask about any limitations on using these items, because they require additional server support.

You can use File Transfer Protocol (FTP) to transfer the files to the server, or you can use the File/Save As command to save the file to the Web. Using the Save As command makes the process quick and easy. The program simply asks you to select the files or directories you want to upload (publish) to a remote server and the location of the server.

LAB REVIEW

Key Terms

absolute link (IE174)
alignment (IE160)
anchor (IE176)
author (IE154)
background (IE163)
bookmark (IE176)
Clip Art (IE171)

external link (IE174)
fixed font (IE159)
fixed link (IE174)
font (IE159)
point (IE159)
publish (IE179)
relative link (IE174)

sizing handle (IE168)
tag (IE156)
typeface (IE159)
variable font (IE159)
wallpaper (IE163)

Command Summary

Command	Shortcut Key	Button	Action
File/**N**ew	Ctrl + N		Creates new Web page
File/**O**pen	Ctrl + O	📂	Opens existing HTML file in FrontPage Express or in Internet Explorer
File/**S**ave	Ctrl + S	💾	Saves file using same file name
File/Save **A**s			Saves current file to new file or uploads to server
File/**P**rint	Ctrl + P	🖨	Prints document
File/E**x**it		✖	Exits program
Edit/**B**ookmark			Creates or edits a bookmark
Edit/**U**nlink			Removes selected hyperlink
Edit/Image Proper**ti**es	Alt + ↵Enter		Accesses features to edit image properties
View/**F**orms toolbar			Hides or displays Forms toolbar

Command	Shortcut Key	Button	Action
View/Format **M**arks			Hides or displays formatting symbols
View/**H**TML			Displays HTML code of current page
Insert/Horizontal **L**ine			Inserts horizontal line across page
Insert/**I**mage		[image button]	Adds image to page
Insert/Hyperlin**k**	Ctrl+K	[image button]	Creates hypertext link
Format/**F**ont/**C**olor		[image button]	Changes text color of selection
Format/**F**ont/F**o**nt Style/Bold Italic		**B** *I*	Applies bold and italics to selection
Format/**P**aragraph		(None)	Applies predefined paragraph style
Format/**P**aragraph/Paragraph **A**lignment		[align buttons]	Changes position of lines between margins
Format/Bullets and **N**umbering		[list button]	Creates bulleted or numbered list of selected text
Format/Bac**k**ground			Changes color of text and background

Matching

1. Match the following with their definition or function.

1. [globe icon] _____ **a.** how text is positioned between margins
2. bookmark _____ **b.** creates bulleted list of selected text
3. external link _____ **c.** identifies file location by its full address
4. [list icon] _____ **d.** color or design displayed behind text on a Web page
5. tags _____ **e.** hyperlink to a document on another Web site
6. alignment _____ **f.** embedded codes that supply information about a Web page
7. wallpaper _____ **g.** an image, pattern, or texture that is used as a background
8. background _____ **h.** creating a Web page
9. authoring _____ **i.** creates link in Web page
10. absolute link _____ **j.** used to create a link to a page on the same Web site

Creating Web Pages

Fill-In Questions

1. Complete the following statements by filling in the blanks with the correct terms.

   a. _____ and _____ are elements that can be added to a Web page to make it attractive and easy to use.

   b. Embedded codes that supply information about the Web page's structure, appearance, and contents are called _____.

   c. A(n) _____ is a specific character design.

   d. _____ can be applied to text to add emphasis or interest to a page.

   e. A(n) _____ is used to create a link to a location in your Web site.

   f. Links to a Web page outside your Web site are _____ links.

   g. A(n) _____ is displayed behind the text to enhance the appearance of a page.

   h. Viewing the page source displays the _____ of the current page.

   i. _____ surround a graphic when it is selected.

   j. Unless otherwise specified, Web images are saved in _____ format.

Discussion Questions

1. Discuss three attributes of a well-designed Web page.
2. Discuss how images are saved in an HTML document.
3. Discuss the two types of hyperlinks and when they would be used.
4. Discuss how to get your Web page on the Internet.

Hands-On Practice Exercises

Step by Step

Rating System Easy / Moderate / Difficult

1. FrontPage Express provides a Personal Home Page Wizard with which to create your own custom Web page. You will use this wizard to create a Web page about yourself.

   a. Start FrontPage Express and from the File menu choose New/Personal Home Page Wizard.

   b. Read the explanation on how to use a wizard.

   c. Follow the instructions and create a page for yourself.

   d. Continue to enhance your page by adding lines and text enhancements as you learned in this lab. Use the search tools you learned about in earlier labs to find pictures and graphics to use on your page. (Remember that many pictures are copyright protected, so do not publish your page without getting permission from the owner.)

   e. Create links to other Web pages that are of interest to you. Include a target link to a particular location within your page.

   f. Print your final Web page.

2. In this problem you will create a home page for a business of your choice.

  a. Plan the design of the home page for the business you have selected. You may want to visit other business home pages on the Web to get an idea of what you like and do not like for your page.

  b. Develop the text of your business home page and type it directly into a new FrontPage Express document window.

  c. Add appropriate paragraph and character formatting.

  b. Add a background.

  c. Add horizontal lines, pictures, and animation to your home page. Use the search tools you learned about in earlier labs to find pictures and graphics to use on your page. (Remember that many pictures are copyright protected, so do not publish your page without getting permission from the owner.)

  d. Create links to other Web pages that are related to the business you selected. Include a target link to a particular location within your page.

  e. Include your name on the page. Save and print your business Web page.

3. You have been asked you to help create a Web page for Call Animation Studio. This studio helps independent graphic designers promote their animated drawings.

  a. Design a home page for the Call Animation Studio.

  b. Include appropriate paragraph and character formatting.

  c. Add a background, lines, and pictures of animation characters to the page to add interest. Use the search tools you learned about in earlier labs to find pictures and graphics to use on your page. Hint: Search on pictures +animation to find animation files. (Remember that many pictures are copyright protected, so do not publish your page without getting permission from the owner.)

  d. Create a second page that includes links to Web pages containing information about computer animation.

  e. Format the second page appropriately.

  f. Add links on both pages to access the other page.

  g. Print the pages you created.

4. As vice president of a club on campus, you have decided to create several Web pages of information about your club.

  a. Plan the design of your club's home page and two additional pages of information. You may want to visit other clubs' home pages on the Web to get an idea of what you like and do not like for your page.

  b. Develop the text of your home page and type it directly into the FrontPage Express window.

  c. Add appropriate paragraph and character formatting.

  d. Add a background.

  e. Add lines, pictures, and animation to your page. Use the search tools you learned about in earlier labs to find pictures and graphics to use on your page. (Remember that many pictures are copyright protected, so do not publish your page without getting permission from the owner.)

  f. Create two additional pages that include more information on the club (such as a calendar of events or status of current projects).

  g. Format the pages appropriately.

  h. Add links on all pages to access the other pages.

  i. Create links to other club Web pages at your school or another school.

  j. Include your name on the home page. Print all three pages.

Concept Summary

Creating Web Pages

Web Page Design

Many elements can be added to a Web page to make it attractive and easy to use. Graphic objects, images, art, and color are perhaps the most important features of Web pages.

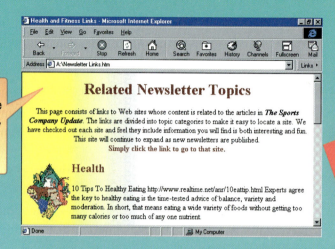

HTML Tags

HTML tags are embedded codes that supply information about the page's structure, appearance, and contents.

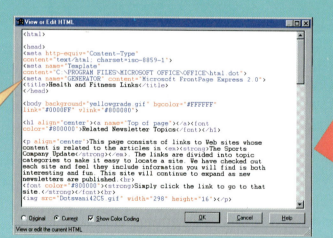

Absolute and Relative Links

When you create a hyperlink in a Web page, you can make the path to the destination of the hyperlink an absolute link or a relative link.

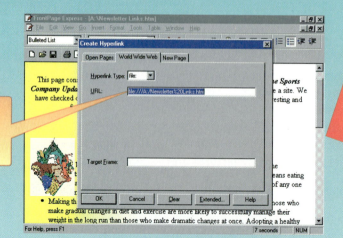

Font

A font, also commonly referred to as a typeface, is a set of characters with a specific design.

Paragraph Alignment

Alignment is how text is positioned on a line between the margins or indents. There are three types of paragraph alignment: left, center, and right.

Character Effects

Different character effects such as bold, italics, and color can be applied to selections to add emphasis or interest to a page.

Concepts

- Web Page Design
- HTML Tags
- Font
  Paragraph Alignment
  Character Effects
- Images
- Absolute and Relative Links

Images

Authors use images in Web pages to provide information or decoration, or to communicate their personal or organization's style.

Appendix

Additional Internet Tools: FTP and Telnet

As the Internet has developed, some programs that were initially used to access information on the Internet have been replaced by new programs and procedures. Others have become an integral part of the browser programs. However, in your travels over the Internet you will still come across these programs and will need to understand and, in some cases, know how to use them to access information.

File Transfer Protocol

Using Internet Explorer you have viewed Web pages that are downloaded to your computer and can be saved as files to a disk. These links begin with http, indicating the protocol that is used to transfer the file. Many other files that you will encounter, such as software applications, graphic images, or very large text files, cannot be viewed by Internet Explorer but can only be downloaded and saved to your disk. These links commonly begin with ftp, indicating that the protocol used to transfer files between computers is **File Transfer Protocol,** or **FTP,** and that the files are stored on FTP servers rather than HTTP servers.

FTP sites, called **archives** or **repositories,** are located on computers throughout the Internet. Many sites are public, meaning anyone can download the files contained on the site to their computer. They may require a password, usually the word "anonymous," before access is granted. For that reason these sites are commonly called anonymous FTP archive sites. FTP sites are usually text based with minimal formatting and appear as a hierarchy of directories/folders and files.

One of the main reasons for the need to download files using FTP is the incorporation of complicated animation, audio, movies, and 3-D virtual reality in Web pages. Although Internet Explorer can display many of these types of files, it is often necessary to obtain special viewer or software enhancement applications to display them. Many of these applications can be obtained from the Internet and installed on your computer to run in conjunction with Internet Explorer. They are commonly divided into two categories: shareware and freeware. **Shareware** are software programs you can try before buying. If you like it, a fee is requested for using it. When you pay and register as a licensed user, you are informed of upgrades as they happen. **Freeware,** also called public domain software, are programs that are available on the Internet without a fee for use. Many freeware programs are used to enhance Internet Explorer's ability to view or play media files. These include plug-ins and helper applications.

Plug-ins are applications that supplement the capabilities of Internet Explorer. Plug-in tools automatically detect the non-HTML components of a page, such as sound or video, and automatically load and run while you are viewing the page. Many plug-ins are automatically installed with Internet Explorer, such as Apple's Quicktime video, which plays movie files with .qt, .mov, and .moov file extensions. Others, however, can be downloaded and added to the Internet Explorer plug-in folder. Some common plug-in tools are listed in the table below.

Plug-in	Runs: File Extension
Live3D, Community Place, WIRL 1.2	Virtual Reality: wrl
MidPlug, Live Audio, VivoActive	Sound: au, aiff, wav, midi
LiveVideo	Microsoft video: avi
Bamba (IBM)	Audio-video streaming tool

Helper applications (also commonly referred to as helper apps) are stand-alone programs that play sound and video files. Helper applications expand Internet Explorer's ability to interpret and display different kinds of files that the standard plug-ins cannot. Once a helper app is installed on your system and you show Internet Explorer where it is located, it will load automatically when needed to run a file. To keep track of the file formats requiring helper applications, Internet Explorer maintains a mapping between file formats and helper applications. When Internet Explorer retrieves a file with a format that Internet Explorer itself cannot read, the application looks at the mapping to find the appropriate application capable of handling the file format. Some helper applications are described in the table on the next page.

> Streaming programs allow an audio or video file to be played while the file is downloaded.

> Because plug-ins operate seamlessly within Internet Explorer, they are often preferred to helper apps. Many helper applications are being converted to plug-ins. If you have the choice, download a plug-in instead of a helper app.

Helper App	Runs
Decompression	
PKZip	Compresses and decompresses files.
WINZip	Compresses and decompresses files.
Animation	
Shockwave www.macromedia.com/shockwave	Plays files created in Macromedia Director, a popular animation creation and authoring tool.
Enliven www.enliven.com	Converts Director movies into streaming files that start to play after a short buffer period.
Streaming Audio	
RealPlayer www.realaudio.com	Combines superior audio quality with streaming video.
TrueSpeech www.dspg.com	High-quality audio.
Liquid MusicPlayer www.liquidaudio.com	Used to sample music over the Internet.
Streaming Video	
VivoActive www.vivo.com	Non-scalable streaming video.

Although there are special FTP programs that you can use to transfer files, Internet Explorer has very conveniently included this feature in the browser. Internet Explorer lets you access FTP servers in the same way you access World Wide Web (HTTP) servers. It handles the interface to the FTP server and the entry of the password automatically for you. On the surface, downloading an FTP file using Internet Explorer appears no different than saving a Web page or image you are viewing. You can also upload files to a site on another computer; however, you must first have permission from the site to upload.

The procedure to download FTP files is the same regardless of whether the file is text, video, audio, or image.

1. Locate the file to download.
   - Use a specialized FTP search engine such as Archie, which indexes FTP sites throughout the Internet. Filez, FTPSearch95, Snoopie, Jumbo, Shareware.com, and Download.com are other sources.
   - Alternatively, you can go directly to an FTP server by typing the FTP URL in the location field.

2. Click on the link to the name of the file you want to download. This starts the Internet Explorer procedure to download and save the file.

3. After a file is downloaded, you may need to expand it using a decompression program on your computer before you can use it. Most large files you download will be compressed (zipped) files. **Compression programs** shrink files so that they are smaller and thereby quicker to transfer between computers. Then you decompress (unzip) the file to expand it before using it. Some compressed files are self-extracting, meaning they decompress automatically when opened.
4. If the file is a software program, install the program, then run it. If it is a text, video, or audio file, open the file to view or hear content using the appropriate type of program, such as a word processor for text or sound or video helper applications for audio or movies.

Using FTP

C/Net's Shareware.com site is a great place to locate software to download. It breaks the index of FTP files into categories for quicker search retrieval. Or you can type in a keyword to search on if you know the name of the item you want to download. It also includes a Most Popular category and a New Arrivals category. You will use this site to download a screen saver program—a program that displays animated pictures on your screen after a period of inactivity.

- If necessary, start Internet Explorer and establish your Internet connection.
- Type **shareware.com** in the Address text box.
- Press ⏎Enter.

Your screen should be similar to Figure A-1.

The Most Popular link lists the 30 top downloads, and the New Arrivals link lists the newest downloads.

FIGURE A-1

lists the newest downloads

- Type **screen saver** in the Search For text box.
- Click Search.
- Scroll the window to see the list of results.

Your screen should be similar to Figure A-2.

FIGURE A-2

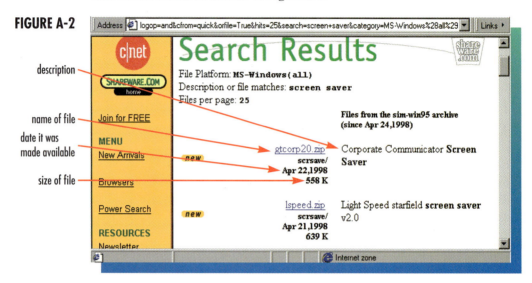

description
name of file
date it was made available
size of file

A list of screen saver files is displayed. It includes a brief description of the file, the date it was made available, and the file size. The files are listed in date order. You will select a file to download to your data disk. When you select a file, note the size of the file.

- Click on any screen saver file link that is of interest to you.

Your screen should be similar to Figure A-3.

Make sure the file you download is not larger than the capacity of your disk.

This text uses the Dreamscope screen saver.

available FTP sites categorized by country

FIGURE A-3

reliability rating of site

This window lists the sites from which you can download the file. Popular files are often located on more than one machine. These multiple sites are called "mirror" sites. The sites are listed in order of reliability (site accessibility and file availability) and are categorized by country. It is suggested that you use the first listed site that is close to your location so that the transfer is as fast as possible.

- Click on a link to an appropriate site for your location.
- Insert a disk in the appropriate drive for your system.
- If necessary, select Save This File to Disk.
- Click [OK].
- In the Save As dialog box, change the location to the drive containing your data disk.
- Click [Save] to save the file to your data disk using the default file name.

As the transfer is made, the File Download dialog box shows the degree of completion. If a transfer is taking too long, you can click [Cancel] to halt the transfer at any time.

> If an informational dialog box appears advising you the file is too large, click [OK] and go back and select another screen saver.

- After the file download is complete, click [OK].
- Check the size of the file to verify that the downloaded file on your disk is the same size as the original file. If not, try again.
- If you are not continuing, exit Internet Explorer and disconnect from the Internet.

> Use Windows Explorer to check the file size.

Once download is complete, you can unzip the file using an appropriate utility program such as PKZip or WinZip. Then read the read.me file that is commonly included on how to use the software and follow the directions to install or set up the program. If it is a self-extracting file, simply double-click on the file name to unzip and install it.

Telnet

Through Internet Explorer you can also communicate directly to other computers on the Internet using Telnet. **Telnet** is an application that allows you to log on and communicate from your local personal computer to a remote computer. After logging on to a remote computer, you can run programs on that computer by typing single-line commands or by selecting from a menu.

Using Telnet

You will use Telnet to communicate with a library and search for books and information on computer crime. Why would you want to browse a library you cannot physically visit? Many libraries share books, so if yours does not have what you want, you can tell the librarian where to get it. Or if you live in an area where the libraries are not yet online, you can use Telnet to do some basic bibliographic research before you go to your local branch. Several hundred libraries around the world, including the Library of Congress, are available to you through Telnet. You will connect to the University of Minnesota library.

- If necessary, start Internet Explorer and establish your Internet connection.
- In the Address text box type **telnet://pubinfo.ais.umn.edu**
- Press **←Enter**.

Your screen should be similar to Figure A-4.

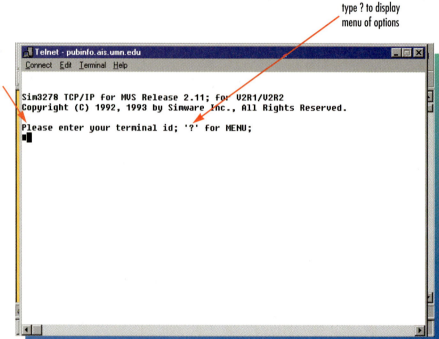

FIGURE A-4

directions on how to continue

type ? to display menu of options

The connection is made, and a Telnet window is opened. You are now communicating directly with another computer and have established a constant connection to this computer. Information on how to proceed is displayed. You will display the menu of terminal options.

- Type **?**
- Press **←Enter**.

> If the ? you typed is not displayed on your screen, choose **T**erminal/**P**references/Local **E**cho/ OK to display characters as you type.

> During a Telnet session, you must press **←Enter** after typing your command to send it to the other computer.

Your screen should be similar to Figure A-5.

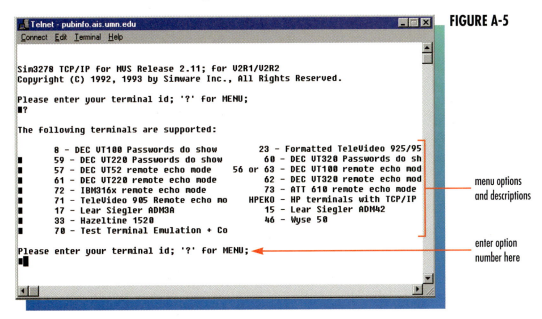

FIGURE A-5

This screen lists the different terminal options as menu selections. Dec VT100 is one of the most common.

- Type **8** (or the appropriate menu option for your system).
- Press ←Enter.

Your screen should be similar to Figure A-6.

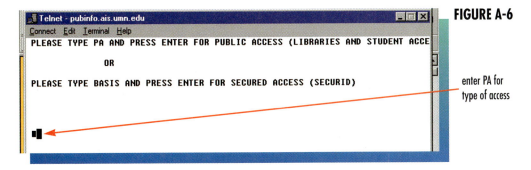

FIGURE A-6

In this window you enter the login access word. Following the instructions on the screen, to enter the public access login password,

- Type **pa**
- Press ←Enter.

Next you will enter a series of commands to connect with the University of Minnesota Library. Again, instructions on how to proceed are included (at the bottom of the screen). You will find that different locations you access using Telnet have different appearances and different procedures. Usually there is a Help command that provides instructions on basic navigational procedures and directions on how to exit the Telnet session.

- Type **1** (to select University Libraries).
- Press [←Enter].
- Type **mncat** (to go to the catalog).
- Press [←Enter].

Your screen should be similar to Figure A-7.

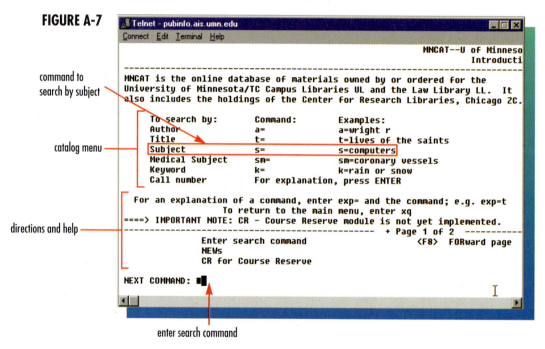

FIGURE A-7

The main catalog menu of options is displayed. You will conduct a search to locate books on computer viruses.

- Type **s=computer viruses**
- Press [←Enter].

Your screen should be similar to Figure A-8.

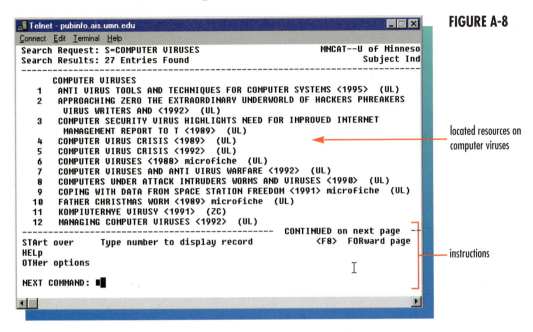

FIGURE A-8

located resources on computer viruses

instructions

A listing of resources containing information on the subject you requested is displayed. The total number of found resources appears at the top of the list.

- Type a number to see more information about a listing.
- Press ⏎Enter.

Your screen should be similar to Figure A-9.

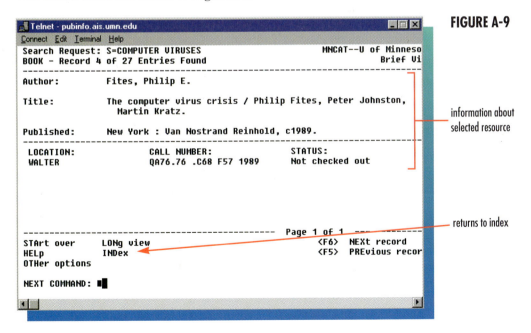

FIGURE A-9

information about selected resource

returns to index

When you are done reading the information on your screen, to return to the index again,

- Type **ind**
- Press ⏎Enter.
- Select other menu items to see what type of information they contain.

When you are done exploring the catalog, to quit the Telnet session,

- Choose **C**onnect/E**x**it.
- Exit Internet Explorer and disconnect from the Internet.

LAB REVIEW

Key Terms

archive   (IE186)
compression program   (IE189)
freeware   (IE187)
FTP   (IE186)
helper application   (IE187)
plug-in   (IE187)
repository   (IE186)
shareware   (IE187)
Telnet   (IE191)

Matching

1. Match the following with their definition or function.

1) shareware _____ **a.** an FTP site
2) freeware _____ **b.** software programs you can try before buying
3) Telnet _____ **c.** software programs that supplement Internet Explorer
4) archive _____ **d.** used to download and upload files
5) plug-in _____ **e.** stand-alone programs that play sound and video
6) FTP _____ **f.** programs available on the Internet without a fee
7) helper app _____ **g.** used to communicate directly with a remote computer

Discussion Questions

1. What is FTP?
2. What does Telnet allow you to do?
3. How does an FTP site differ from a Telnet site?
4. How do plug-ins differ from helper apps?

Hands-On Practice Exercises

Step by Step

Rating System
★ Easy
★★ Moderate
★★★ Difficult

1. Locate a software program of interest to you and download it to your data disk. Check the size of the file before you download it to insure you have enough disk space.

2. Telnet to the Library of Congress (telnet://locis.loc.gov) and search for a book using the author's name.

3. Telnet to the IRS (telnet://iris.irs.ustreas.gov) and see what information they have available. How up-to-date is this information? Do they have a WWW site?

4. Locate a shareware or freeware game program of interest to you and download it. Execute the program and write a short description of how the game is played and what additional features are available for purchase, if any. Check the size of the file before you download it to insure you have enough disk space.

5. You are preparing a paper for a course in your field of study. Use Telnet to locate three books that contain information on the topic of your paper. Write down the author, edition, and title as they appear and write a brief summary of how you found the books and at what library you located them. Note: You may be able to Telnet to your school's library.

Glossary of Key Terms

Glossary of Key Terms

Absolute link: A link that identifies the file location of the destination by its full address.

Address book: A file that contains a collection of names and e-mail addresses that you use frequently.

Alias: A shortcut for a URL or e-mail address.

Alignment: How text is positioned on a line between the margins or indents.

Anchor: See bookmark.

Archive: To save e-mail messages. Also, an FTP site on an FTP server.

Article: A message posted to a newsgroup.

Attachment: A text or graphic file that is attached to an e-mail message.

Author: To create a Web page.

Background: A color or design that is displayed behind the contents of a Web page.

Bitnet: An academic network founded in 1981 to link universities by e-mail.

Bookmark: A marked location within a Web site to which you can create a link.

Boolean operator: Special words that indicate a relationship among the keywords in a search. The most common are AND, OR, and NOT.

Browser: A program used to access and display WWW pages, to access FTP sites, and to provide an interface to the Internet and WWW documents.

Cache: An area on your computer system where copies of Web pages are stored when they are downloaded.

Certificate: A tamper-resistant file used for security purposes that identifies the individual to whom it is issued and includes public and private keys.

Channel: An area where chat discussions take place. Also called a chat room.

Chat group: A method of communication over the Internet that allows people to converse in real time.

Chat room: See channel.

Clip art: Simple graphic files that are usually bundled with a software application.
Compression program: An application that shrinks and expands files.
Content frame: A frame that displays the contents of the selected page.
Decryption: The code used to unscramble an encrypted message.
Digital signature: Ensures that a message was actually sent by the sender, not from an impersonator.
Discussion group: A form of Internet communication that allows you to participate in interactive, ongoing discussions about a topic of common interest with people from all over the world.
Domain Name System (DNS): The e-mail addressing system used on the Internet.
Download: To copy a file to your computer from a remote site.
Eavesdrop: A security invasion in which a third party listens in on a private conversation.
E-mail: Electronic mail; a message that is sent between users on the Internet.
Emoticon: See smiley.
Encryption: The code used to scramble a message so that no one can read the message except people who have the correct decryption code.
External link: A hyperlink to a file on another Web site.
FAQ: Documents that include answers to frequently asked questions.
Favorite: Permanently stores the URL of a page so that you can easily retrieve the page again.
File Transfer Protocol (FTP): A system of rules for transferring files across the Internet.
Fixed font: A font where each character takes up the same amount of space.
Fixed link: See absolute link.
Flame: To send inflammatory remarks in an e-mail message.
Flame war: Ongoing thread of inflammatory e-mail messages.
Followed link: A link that you have recently accessed.
Font: Set of characters with a specific design.
Form: Used to enter and submit information to a Web site.
Forward: To pass a message along to another e-mail address.
Frame: A rectangular division of the browser's display that contains a separate, scrollable page.
Frame set: A special Web page that defines the size and location of each frame within the set of frames.
Freeware: Programs available on the Internet that do not require a fee for use.
Gateway: A computer that translates e-mail messages from the protocol used on one network to that used on another network.
Helper application: Stand-alone program that expands the browser's capability to play sound and video files that the standard plug-ins cannot.
Hierarchy: A category of newsgroups.
History list: A list of locations you have accessed during your current Explorer session.
Home page: The first page of information for a Web site.
Hyperlink: See hypertext link.

Hypertext link: A connection to another Web page or location on the current page.
HyperText Markup Language (HTML): The programming language used to create Web pages.
Impersonation: A security invasion in which a sender or receiver uses a false identity for communication.
Inline image: An image that loads automatically when a Web page is displayed.
Internet: A network of thousands of computer networks that allows computers to communicate with each other.
Internet Message Access Protocol (IMAP): A protocol used by the incoming mail server to deliver messages to your mailbox.
Internet relay chat (IRC): A program that allows simultaneous participation in a discussion over a particular internet channel.
Internet Service Provider (ISP): A company that provides access to the Internet for a fee.
Keyword search: A method of searching by which you enter a word, words, or phrase that the search program will compare to some part of the text it has stored in the database to locate the information you are seeking.
Link: See hypertext link.
List address: E-mail address used to participate in mailing list discussions.
Listserv address: E-mail address used to subscribe to a mailing list. Also called a subscription address.
Listserver (listserv): The program used to send e-mail to and from mailing list subscribers.
Lurk: To read messages without posting to the newsgroup or mailing list.
Mailbox: An area on the mail server that is used to store e-mail messages.
Mailer program: Program that provides the means of creating, sending, and reading e-mail messages. Also called a reader program.
Mailing list: A discussion group in which e-mail messages are sent directly to the e-mail addresses of every subscriber.
Mail server: A computer on the Internet used for storing e-mail messages.
Main window: The area of the Internet Explorer window that displays the pages of information.
Manipulation: A security invasion in which a message is intercepted and changed.
Metasearch engine: A search utility that submits your request to multiple search engines simultaneously.
Moderated: Discussion group where postings are reviewed by a moderator before being forwarded to the entire group.
Netiquette: The standard rules of courteous electronic communication.
Newsgroup: A discussion group in which e-mail messages are posted to the newsgroup site, where they can be accessed by anyone who subscribes to the newsgroup.
Newsgroup site: A computer that participates in the Usenet network where newsgroup messages are stored.
Newsreader program: A software program used to access, read, and organize newsgroup messages.

News server: See newsgroup site.

Nickname: A complete or shortened name used to identify a recipient of e-mail.

Plug-in: Program that supplements the browser's capability to play sound and video. It loads automatically and runs while you are viewing the page.

Point: Unit of measurement for the height and width of characters.

Point to Point Protocol (PPP): Creates an Internet connection that checks data transfer over lines and sends it again if damaged.

Post: To send a message to a newsgroup or mailing list.

Post Office Protocol (POP): A protocal used by the incoming mail server to deliver messages to your mailbox.

Private key: The decryption code that is provided with the certificate and used to unscramble messages you receive.

Protocol: A set of rules that control how software and hardware communicate on a network.

Public key: The encryption code that is provided with the certificate and used to scramble messages you send.

Publish: The process of uploading your Web pages to a server for access by the public.

Quote: To include parts of the original e-mail message in the body of the reply.

Reader program: See mailer program.

Relative link: A link based on a path in which the first part of the path is shared by both the file that contains the hyperlink and the destination file.

Repository: An FTP site on an FTP server.

Rich-text document: A document that includes formatting such as bold and italics.

Router: A switch located at a network intersection on the Internet that determines the best path for a packet to travel to reach its destination.

Search engine: A type of search service that typically offers no editorial content or categories.

Search service: A huge database of Internet sites that is used to locate information on the Web.

Serial Line Internet Protocol (SLIP): A set of rules similar to PPP, but it does not provide damage check.

Server: A computer that holds information, providing it to clients on request.

Shareware: Programs available on the Internet that you can try before buying but which require a fee for continued use.

Shout: To type a message in all uppercase characters.

Signature line: A personalized identification that is added to the end of the body of a message.

Simple Mail Transport Protocol (SMPT): A set of rules used by the outgoing mail server for sending e-mail messages over the Internet.

Sizing handle: One of eight black boxes surrounding a selected object, which indicate that the object can be sized and moved.

Smiley: Picture of smiling or winking face used to add feeling to e-mail.

Startup home page: The Web page Explorer displays when first loaded.

Store-and-forward: A system of mail forwarding that routinely holds messages for later batch sending.

Subscribe: To join a newsgroup or mailing list.
Subscription address: See listserv address.
Tag: Embedded HTML code that supplies information about a Web page's structure, appearance, and contents.
Telnet: An application that allows you to log onto and run programs on remote computers on the Internet.
Thread: A newsgroup discussion about a specific topic with a common theme.
Thumbnail: Miniature image displayed on a page that can be displayed full size by clicking on the image.
Topic search: A method of searching by navigating through a hierarchy of topic listings that group the items in a database into subject categories.
Transmission Control Protocol/Internet Protocol (TCP/IP): The core protocol used to send information on the Internet.
Troll: To deliberately post a message containing incorrect information with the intent of receiving know-it-all replies.
Typeface: See font.
Unfollowed link: A link that you have not recently clicked on or followed.
Uniform Resource Locator (URL): Provides location information that is used to navigate through the Internet to access a particular page.
Unmoderated: Discussion group where postings are not reviewed by a moderator before being forwarded to the entire group.
Upload: To send a file to another computer.
Usenet: The network of newsgroups on the Internet.
Variable font: A font where some letters take up more space than other letters.
Wallpaper: A background image, pattern, or texture.
Web directory: A type of search service that can be searched by topic or subjects. Many include site reviews.
Web page: A document file created using HTML that is stored on a Web server and viewed using a browser.
Web site: A location on a Web server consisting of related Web pages.
White pages: An online database in which you can search for people.
Wizard: A series of dialog boxes that guides you through the completion of a procedure.
World Wide Web (WWW): Part of the Internet that consists of information organized into Web pages containing text and graphic images and hypertext links.
Yellow pages: An online database in which you search for businesses.

Command Summary

Command	Shortcut Key	Button	Action
Internet Explorer			
File/**O**pen	Ctrl+O		Opens a Web page
File/Save **A**s			Saves current page to disk
File/**P**rint		🖨	Prints current page or frame
File/**C**lose		✖	Exits Internet Explorer
View/**T**oolbars			Hides or displays selected toolbar
View/**T**oolbars/**T**ext Labels			Hides or displays labels on Standard Buttons toolbar
View/**E**xplorer Bar/**S**earch		🔍	Opens Search Explorer bar
View/**E**xplorer Bar/**F**avorites		⭐	Displays Favorites bar
View/**E**xplorer Bar/**H**istory		🕘	Displays History bar
View/Sto**p**	Esc	✖	Stops loading of a page
View/**R**efresh	F5	🔄	Reloads current page
View/Sour**c**e			Displays HTML code for current page
View/**F**ull Screen		🗖	Switches between normal view and full screen view
View/Internet **O**ptions/General/**S**ettings			Changes settings associated with cache
View/Internet **O**ptions/Security			Changes security settings
View/Internet **O**ptions/Advanced/ Multimedia/Show Picture			Turns on and off display of inline image

Command Summary

Command	Shortcut Key	Button	Action
Go/**B**ack	Alt + ←	Back	Displays last viewed page
Go/**F**orward	Alt + →	Forward	Displays next viewed page after using Back
Go/**H**ome Page		(home)	Displays startup home page
Go/**S**earch the Web			Opens search Web page
F**a**vorites/**A**dd to Favorites			Saves URL of current page
F**a**vorites/**O**rganize Favorites			Organizes Favorites list
Outlook Express			
File/**P**rint	Ctrl + P		Prints selected message
File/E**x**it			Exits Outlook Express
Edit/**D**elete	Ctrl + D		Deletes selected item
Edit/**U**ndelete			Restores deleted item
Edit/Pu**r**ge Deleted Messages			Permanently removes deleted messages
Edit/Mark as U**n**read			Changes message status to unread
Edit/**F**ind Message	Ctrl + Shift + F		Finds messages in current folder
View/Current **V**iew/D**e**leted Messages			Displays messages that have been marked for deletion
View/**C**olumns			Specifies columns to display and location
View/Sort **B**y			Changes column to sort on and order of sort
View/**L**ayout			Changes display of window elements
Go/**G**o to Folder	Ctrl + Y		Selects folder to go to
Go/**N**ews			Opens your news server
Tools/**S**end and Receive	Ctrl + M	Send and Receive	Gets new e-mail messages from server and sends any outgoing e-mail
Tools/**A**ddress Book	Ctrl + Shift + B	(book)	Opens address book
Tools/**A**ccounts/**A**dd/**M**ail			Configures Outlook Express mail
Tools/S**t**ationery/**S**ignature			Creates a signature line
Tools/**O**ptions			Specifies configuration settings
Tools/Download **t**his newsgroup			Displays messages in selected newsgroup

Command Summary **IE207**

Command	Shortcut Key	Button	Action
Tools/News**g**roups		News groups	Subscribes to selected newsgroup
Tools/Unsubscr**i**be from this newsgroup			Unsubscribes from selected newsgroup
Compose/**N**ew Message	Ctrl + N	Compose Message / Compose Message	Creates new e-mail or newsgroup message
Compose/Reply to Newsgr**o**up	Ctrl + G	Reply to Group	Sends message back to newsgroup
Compose/**R**eply to Author	Ctrl + R	Reply to Author	Returns e-mail or newsgroup message to sender's address
Compose/**F**orward	Ctrl + F	Forward Message	Sends e-mail or newsgroup message to new address
Compose/**C**ancel Message			Removes message you posted to newsgroup
New Message Window			
File/S**e**nd Message	Alt + S	Send / Post	Sends message immediately to e-mail recipient or discussion group
File/Send **L**ater			Stores message in Outbox to be sent later
Edit/**U**ndo	Ctrl + Z		Reverses last action or command
Edit/Cu**t**	Ctrl + X		Cuts selected text to Clipboard
Edit/**C**opy	Ctrl + C		Copies selected text to Clipboard
Edit/**P**aste	Ctrl + V		Pastes text from Clipboard
Edit/Select **A**ll	Ctrl + A		Selects entire document
Insert/File **A**ttachment			Attaches file to e-mail
F**o**rmat/**F**ont/**S**tyle/Italic	Ctrl + I	*I*	Italicizes selected text
F**o**rmat/**F**ont/**S**tyle/Bold	Ctrl + B	**B**	Bolds selected text
Tools/**S**pelling	F7		Starts spell-checking feature
Tools/Select **R**ecipients			Selects recipients from address book
FrontPage Express			
File/**N**ew	Ctrl + N		Creates a new Web page
File/**O**pen	Ctrl + O		Opens existing HTML file in FrontPage Express or in Internet Explorer

INTERNET EXPLORER 4

Command Summary

Command	Shortcut Key	Button	Action
File/**S**ave	Ctrl + S	💾	Saves file using same file name
File/Save **A**s			Saves current file to a new file or uploads to server
File/**P**rint	Ctrl + P	🖨	Prints document
File/E**x**it		✖	Exits program
Edit/**B**ookmark			Creates or edits a bookmark
Edit/U**n**link			Removes selected hyperlink
Edit/Image Propert**i**es	Alt + Enter		Accesses features to edit image properties
View/F**o**rms Toolbar			Hides or displays Forms toolbar
View/Format **M**arks			Hides or displays formatting symbols
View/**H**TML			Displays HTML code of current page
Insert/Horizontal **L**ine			Inserts horizontal line across page
Insert/**I**mage		🖼	Adds image to page
Insert/Hyperlin**k**	Ctrl + K	🌐	Creates hypertext link
F**o**rmat/**F**ont/**C**olor		🎨	Changes text color of selection
F**o**rmat/**F**ont/F**o**nt Style/Bold Italic		**B** *I*	Applies bold and italics to selection
F**o**rmat/**P**aragraph		[None] ▼	Applies predefined paragraph style
F**o**rmat/**P**aragraph/Paragraph **A**lignment		☰ ☰ ☰	Changes position of lines between margins
F**o**rmat/Bullets and **N**umbering		☷	Creates bulleted or numbered list of selected text
F**o**rmat/Bac**k**ground			Changes color of text and background

Index

Entries with page numbers in **boldface** refer to glossary definitions.

. (dot), 79
. (period), 79
& (AND operator), 59
/ (forward slash), 15
− (minus sign), 59
() (parentheses), 59
+ (plus sign), 59
" " (quotation marks), 59
~ (tilde), 15
* (wildcard), 59

Abbreviations
    e-mail, 86–87
    newsgroup, 126
Absolute links, 153, 174, 184, **198**
Address bar, 12, 13
Address book, 77, 115, **198**
    creating, 100–102
    deleting entry, 102
Address box, 16
Alias, 17, **198**
Alignment, 153, 160, 185, **198**
All-in-One Search Page, 49
AltaVista, 48
Anchor, 176–178
AND operator, 59
Animation helper apps, 188
AOL NetFind, 48
Archives, 107, 186, **198**

Articles, 118, **198**
Attachment, 84, 94–96, **198**
Audio helper apps, 188
Authoring, 154, **198**
AutoComplete feature, 16

Background, 163–165, **198**
"Big Seven" hierarchies, 120
Bitnet, 133, **198**
Bitnet address, 136
Blink, 161–163
Body, 84, 114
Bold effect, 161–163
Bookmark, 176–178, **198**
Boolean operators, 47, 59, 75, **198**
Bot, 47
Browsers, 2, 5, 9, **198**
Bulleted list, 173–174
Bulletin board systems (BBS), 3
Business, finding, 66–69

Cache, 9, 24, 44, **198**
Campus computer systems, 3–4
Certificate, 34, **198**
Channels, 140, **198**
Character effects, 153, 161–163, 185
Chat groups, 2, 117, 151, **198**
    abbreviations, 140
    joining, 140–142
Chat room; *see* Channels
Clip Art, 171–173, **199**; *see also* Graphics

C/Net, 48, 189
Color; *see* Character effects
Compression programs, 189, **199**
Content frame, 21–22, **199**
Corporate networks, 3
Create Hyperlink dialog box, 177–178

Decompression helper apps, 188
Decryption, 34, **199**
Deleted Items folder, 82
Digital signature, 34, **199**
Discussion groups, 2, 116, 117, **199**; *see also* Chat groups; Mailing lists; Newsgroups
Disk cache, 24
DNS Lookup Failed error message, 16
Domain name, 15
Domain Name System (DNS), 79, **199**
Download, 2, 5, **199**
Drafts folder, 82

Eavesdrop, 34, **199**
E-mail, 1, 5, **199**; *see also* Outlook Express
    abbreviations, 86–87
    address system, 79
    attaching files to, 93–94
    checking incoming, 96–100
    composing messages, 83–89
    defined, 77–78
    emoticons for, 86
    folders, 82
    netiquette, 86–87, 114
    style, 114
E-mail folders, 77, 115
E-mail messages
    body, 114
    checking spelling, 89–90
    composing, 83–89
    deleting, 107–108
    editing, 91
    formatting, 92–93
    forwarding, 104–106
    header, 114
    incoming, 96–100
    parts of, 84, 114
    printing, 108
    replying to, 103–104
    saving, 107
    sending, 94

Emoticons, 86
Encryption, 34, **199**
Etiquette; *see* Netiquette
Excite, 48
Explorer Bar, 25
External links, 174, **199**

FAQs (Frequently Asked Questions), 126, **199**
Favorites, 9, **199**
    creating, 26–29
    organizing, 26–29
File Not Found error message, 16
File Transfer Protocol; *see* FTP (File Transfer Protocol)
Files
    attaching to e-mail, 93–94
    transferring, 2
Fixed fonts, 159, **199**
Fixed link; *see* Absolute link
Flame, 126, **199**
Flame war, 126
Folders, e-mail, 82
Followed link, 20, **199**
Fonts, 153, 159, 185, **199**
Formatting
    e-mail messages, 92–93
    Web pages, 158–160
Forms, 33–35, **199**
Forward, 104–106, **199**
Frame, 9, 21–22, **199**
Frame set, 21, **199**
Freenets, 4
Freeware, 187, **199**
FrontPage Express, 153–154; *see also* Web pages
    adding lines, 171–173
    aligning paragraphs, 160
    creating links, 174–179
    creating Web pages, 157–158
    formatting text, 158–160
    inserting images, 166–169
    previewing, 169–171
    publishing Web pages, 179–180
FTP (File Transfer Protocol), 2, 5, 186, 189–191, **199**
    downloading files, 188–189
    search engines, 188
    sites, 190
Fullscreen view, 17–18

Gateway, 133, **199**
GIF file format, 166
Graphics, 22, 153, 185; *see also* Clip Art
    inserting, 166–169
    saving, 31–32
    sizing, 168
    wrapping text around, 168–169

Harvester, 47
Header, 84, 114
Headings, 159–160
Helper apps, 187–188, **199**
Hierarchy, 120, **199**
History list, 23–26, **199**
Home page, 11, **199**
HotBot, 48
HTML (HyperText Markup Language), 9, 30–31, 157–158
HTML tags, 153, 184
Hyperlinks; *see* Links
Hypertext links; *see* Links
HyperText Markup Language (HTML), 44, **200**

Icon
    mail, 98
    newsgroup, 122
Image dialog box, 167
Images; *see* Clip Art; Graphics
IMAP (Internt Message Access Protocol), 83
Impersonation, 34, **200**
Inbox folder, 82
Incoming messages, 96–100
Infoseek, 48
Inline image, 22, **200**
Internet, 5, **200**
    connecting to, 3–4
    defined, 1
    uses for, 1–2
Internet Message Access Protocol (IMAP), 83, **200**
Internet Service Provider (ISP), 3, **200**
Internet Yellow Pages (McGraw-Hill), 133
IRC (Internet relay chat), 140, **200**
ISP (Internet Service Provider), 5
Italic, 161–163

JPEG file format, 166

Keyword search, 51, 55–58, 75, **200**
    advanced methods, 58–63
LAN (local area network), 3
Libraries, 4, 191–196
Links, 2, 5, 9, 18, 44, 174–175, 184, **200**
    clicking, 19
    creating, 174–179
    followed, 20
    selecting, 18–23
    unfollowed, 20
Links Bar, 12, 14
List, bulleted, 173–174
List address, 117, 135–136, 151, **200**
Lists; *see* Mailing lists
Listserv(er), 133, **200**
    address, 135
    commands, 137
Logo, Internet Explorer, 12
LookSmart, 48
Lurking, 130, **200**
Lycos, 48
Lycos PointCom, 48

Mail; *see* E-mail; Outlook Express
Mail icon, 98
Mail server, 77, 83, 114, **200**
Mailbox, 77, **200**
Mailer program, 77, **200**
Mailing lists, 2, 5, 100, 117, 151, **200**
    addresses, 136
    etiquette, 139
    finding, 132–135
    subscribing, 135–140
Main window, **200**
Manipulation, 34, **200**
Memory cache, 24
Menu bar, 11–12
Messages; *see* E-mail messages
Metasearch engines, 47, 63–65, 74, **200**; *see also* Search engines
Microsoft Internet Explorer
    browser window features, 9–15
    company logo, 12, 16
    full version, 5
    search services, 49–51
    standard version, 4

Mirror sites, 191
Moderated newsgroups, 118, **200**

Near operator, 59
NetGuide, 48
Netiquette, 86–87, 114, **200**
    mailing list, 139
    newsgroups, 126
New Message window, 83
News server, 118
Newsgroup culture, 117, 150
Newsgroup icon, 122
Newsgroup site, 118, **200**
Newsgroups, 2, 5, 117, 150, **200**
    abbreviations, 126
    etiquette, 126
    finding and subscribing to, 119–122
    hierarchies, 120, 150
    posting messages to, 125–130
    reading messages, 123–125
    replying to, 130
    searching for topics, 131–132
    types, 118
    unsubscribing, 131
Newsreader program, 118–122, **200**
Nickname, 100, **201**
NotePad utility, 31

OR operator, 59
Outbox folder, 82
Outlook Express, 77; *see also* E-mail
    newsreader program, 118–122
    setting up, 78–83

Page Properties dialog box, 163–164
Paragraph alignment, 153, 160, 185
Path name, 15
People, finding, 66–69
Plain text file, 32
Plug-ins, 187, **201**
Points, 159, **201**
POP (Post Office Protocol), 83, **201**
Post, 118, **201**
PPP (Point to Point Protocol), 3, 5, **201**
Printing
    e-mail message, 108
    Web pages, 35–36

Private key, 34, **201**
Protocols, 2–3, 5, **201**
    part of URL, 15
Public domain software, 187
Public key, 34, **201**
Publish, 179, **201**; *see also* FrontPage Express;
    Web pages

Quote, 100, **201**

Reader, **201**
Reader program, 77, **201**
Relative links, 153, 174, 184, **201**
Replying, to e-mail message, 103–104
Repositories, 186, **201**
RFD (Request for Discussion), 126
Rich-text documents, 92, **201**
Robot, 47
Routers, 3, 5, **201**

Saint, 126
Saving
    e-mail message, 107
    images, 31–32
    Web pages, 31–32
SavvySearch, 63–65
Scroll bar, 17
Search engines, 47, **201**; *see also* Metasearch engines
    FTP, 188
Search methods, 47
Search services, 74, **201**
    accessing, 47–51
    defined, 47
    Usenet, 118, 202
Searching
    advanced methods, 58–63
    keyword, 51, 55–58, 75
    topic, 51–55, 75
Security, 9, 34
Security zones, 34
Sent Items folder, 82
Serial Line Internet Protocol (SLIP), 3, **201**
Server, 11, **201**
Server Error message, 16
Server name, 15
Shareware, 187, **201**
Shareware.com site, 189–191

Shortcuts; *see* Standard Buttons toolbar
Shouting, 87, **201**
Signature line, 84, **201**
Simple Mail Transport Protocol (SMTP), 83, **201**
Sizing handles, 167–168, **201**
SLIP (Serial Line Internet Protocol), 3, 5
Smileys, 86, **201**
SMTP (Simple Mail Transport Protocol), 83
Spam, 126
Spelling, checking, 89–90
Spider, 47
Standard Buttons toolbar, 12–13
Startup home page, 11, **201**
Status Bar, 14
Store-and-forward technology, 77, **201**
Streaming audio helper apps, 188
Streaming video helper apps, 188
Subscribing
    to newsgroups, 119–122, **202**
    to Web pages, 26
Subscript, 161–163
Subscription address, 117, 135, 151, **202**
Superscript, 161–163

Tagged text, 156
Tags, HTML, 156, **202**
TCP/IP (Transmission Control Protocol/Internet
    Protocol), 3, 5
Telnet, 2, 5, 191–196, **202**
Temporary Internet Files, 24
Text
    aligning, 160
    formatting, 158–160
    wrapping around images, 168–169
Text file, 32
Thread, 117, 124, 150, **202**
Thumbnail image, 22, **202**
Title bar, 11
Toolbar, 12–13
Topic search, 51–55, 75, **202**
Transmission Control Protocol/Internet Protocol
    (TCP/IP), **202**
Trolls, 126, **202**
Typeface; *see* Fonts

Underline, 161–163
Unfollowed link, 20, **202**

Unmoderated newsgroups, 118, **202**
Unzipped files, 189, 191
Upload, 2, 6, **202**
URL (Uniform Resource Locator), 9, 44, **202**
    copying to WordPad, 58
    entering, 15–18
    parts of, 15
Usenet, 118, **202**; *See also* Newsgroups

Variable fonts, 159, **202**
Video helper apps, 188

Wallpaper, 163–165, **202**
Web crawler, 47
Web directories, 47, **202**
Web Guides; *see* Web directories
Web pages, 9, 11, 44, **202**; *see also* FrontPage Express
    adding lines, 171–173
    adding to Favorites list, 26–29
    aligning paragraphs, 160
    applying character effects, 161–163
    creating links, 174–179
    designing, 153–156, 184
    entering content, 156–158
    formatting text, 158–160
    inserting images, 166–169
    previewing, 169–171
    printing, 35–36
    publishing, 179–180
    saving, 31–32
    subscribing to, 26
Web site, 11, **202**
Web (World Wide Web), 2, 6, **202**
WebCrawler search service, 48
White pages, 66–69, **202**
Wildcard, 59
Wizard, 79–81, 126, **202**
WordPad, copying URL to, 58
Worm, 47
Wrapping text, around images, 168–169

Yahoo!, 48, 52–55
Yellow pages, 66–69, **202**

Zipped files, 189

Notes

Notes